DESTINY, FATE

Drive Your
Destiny

CREATE A VISION FOR YOUR LIFE,
BUILD BETTER **HABITS** FOR **WEALTH**
AND **HEALTH**, AND UNLOCK YOUR
INNER **GREATNESS**

By Scott Allan

www.scottallanauthor.com

Contents

"Knowing our personal mission further enhances the flow of mysterious coincidences as we are guided towards our destinies. First we have a question, and then dreams, daydreams, and intuitions lead us towards the answers which are synchronistically provided by the wisdom of another person."

— **James Redfield**, bestselling author of *The Celestine Prophecy*

INTRODUCTION

Drive Your Destiny

Do you feel dissatisfied with your current path in life?
Does your destiny seem like some mundane
existence governed by circumstances beyond your
control? Do you want to be the master of your own path
in life, but you're not sure where to start?

If so, Drive Your Destiny is your blueprint to discovering
the best of who you are and what you have to offer. This
book will teach you the keys to discovering the inner
greatness within you. You will learn to take charge and
direct your actions to work for you instead of against
you. As we will see, neither the circumstances nor the
external conditions decide your fate—you do.

The Force That Changed the Course of My Life

In March of 1997, I made a decision that would change
the course of my life. It was a choice unlike any I had
ever made before. I decided to alter the course of events
controlling my destiny. How had I arrived at this
change?

My life had hit a wall. I was single again, sick of my job
(and not very good at it, anyway) and each day seemed
to melt into the next without any real purpose. I was
drifting. Within me, something struggled to break free. I
wanted more out of life than just punching in, filling in a

time card, and working toward what everyone else called a future.

Until that moment, I had been playing the victim—the victim of circumstances, of limitations, of a life at the mercy of decisions made by others. One day, I revolted. I said, "No more." I decided I could shift the course of my life.

I hated knowing that I had a dream once, and now the dream was as far away as the moon. I was desperate. Worse than that, I learned what one form of suffering really meant: to be living a life completely empty of meaning. To have no purpose other than going to work, paying bills, and complaining to my friends about the unfairness of it all.

I realized in that moment it was up to me to take charge and steer my path toward the future I really wanted.

So, I committed to doing whatever it took to live in a different way. I decided I would no longer drift through life, and instead take charge of my destiny. I wanted to create the path instead of falling into the river of life and letting the current take me.

My life shifted from a menial existence to a destiny I began creating. For the next year, I worked hard to shift my mindset, change my limiting beliefs, and focus on my dream of traveling, writing, and not just being someplace else, but becoming something new.

Was I afraid? Yes. Did I think I would fail? Many times I was filled with uncertainty. I didn't know what the world had in store for me. I doubted I was doing the right thing. But what scared me more was the idea of waking up someday and realizing that I never did anything to gain control over my fears.

Taking action didn't scare me; it was the possibility of not taking action and living with regret that caused me anxiety. I didn't want my destiny to be dictated by a paycheck or a job I didn't enjoy. So, despite the fear I had in deciding to change everything, I set out to create a master plan.

Overcoming fear isn't just about doing what scares you, but having the courage to say no to the things you no longer want. In the months that I prepared myself for my journey, I had several relationship opportunities, job offers that paid well, and the promise of stability and financial security.

But none of that appealed to me. I was being driven by something else that, until years later, I could only describe as a call to destiny. I wanted to experience as much of this life as I could, and the only way to do that was begin making different decisions. This resulted in a different course of action. For the first time in my life, I made choices that I wasn't afraid of. Self-doubt no longer held me back. And, I made a decision that it never would again.

At the end of the day, when I went home at night and worked on my master goals, something told me this was the way to go. Was it the voice of destiny? I didn't know, but whenever I spent time planning the life I wanted, instead of accepting the way things were, I was taken over by a feeling of passion for what I was doing.

This passion was the unbreakable force that pushed me ahead.

We all have the strength within us to be the people we want to be.

There is no such thing as being trapped in a bad situation; you can only be trapped by your thoughts. When you free your mind, you can master any circumstance.

I stayed fixed on my goals for a year, spending my free time reading books and learning about things I had never thought about before. I took language courses for countries I planned to visit. I talked to people about all the things I was going to see and what I would do when I got there. Sometimes they even listened to me. But most of the time I just ended up talking to myself.

Even when a relationship almost held me back, I stayed on course. When friends and family told me to come back to reality, I ignored the warnings and forged ahead. I learned what it means to persist, and the raw power of committing to a single course of action. It was powerful. It overrode my weaker emotions and turned my mind into a focused engine hungry for more.

Then, one day, after months of dreaming and planning, I bought a ticket to the Far East and made my journey real.

Eventually, this journey has brought me to these pages, doing what I love the most: writing about life experiences, how to overcome the fear and hurdles along the way, and helping others to discover their real dreams. I have traveled to most of the places I once dreamed about, and many others are still on my list today.

Walt Disney once said, "All our dreams can come true, if we have the courage to pursue them."

You have that courage, even if you haven't recognized it yet.

Drive Your Destiny is a book that focuses on taking ACTION. In this book, you will discover how to:

- Foster beliefs that shape your destiny.
- Learn to craft a vision for your life that forges the building blocks of your destiny.

- Empower your life with vision-building strategies.
- Develop positive habits.
- Define your dream and create a plan for it.
- Master your passion and develop a mindset for excellence.
- Maximize your health and vitality.
- Build financial success and finance your dream.

Staying fixed on your dream is not always easy. We struggle with life's distractions and circumstances beyond our control on a daily basis. But what I learned is that we don't have to concern ourselves with the events that don't concern us. We can focus on our own path and choose to ignore the noise in the world.

Why I wrote *Drive Your Destiny*

I wrote this book to inspire, encourage, motivate—and most of all—to drive you to take action. I urge you to find that inner greatness, that internal fire, even if the world has tried to convince you it went out years ago.

I can promise you, if you look deep enough, you'll find it again. I know I did. You will, too.

This book is a guide to help you create anything you want in your life. Take out the guesswork and replace uncertainty with clarity. Remove your self-doubt while increasing the self-confidence you never knew you had. Toss out your habit of passive activity and replace it with forward action.

When you combine these elements, you have a formula that works. It isn't complicated and it doesn't have to cause you unneeded stress or pressure. The only real path to success is committing to your plan and then putting into action the right strategies to get where you need to be.

The system I used to take charge of my own destiny is what I will share with you in this book. I am not selling any easy gimmicks or quick fixes. There is no such thing as an instant formula for success. It takes work, diligence, perseverance, and formulating a concrete vision of what you want to do.

It takes time and dealing with the many frustrations of doing everything wrong before you get it right. That is the price of succeeding where most would fail.

How This Book Can Help You...And why You Need to Read It!

As far back as I can remember, I wanted to live a dynamic and inspiring life. I read books about great heroes and people of power and influence who seized their destiny and ran toward success.

What did they have that made them different? For example, how did Abraham Lincoln, even after failing in most aspects of his life, rise to be such an epic figure?

How did Henry Ford create one of the biggest car manufacturing companies in the world? How did Andrew Carnegie build the largest steel company in the world and subsequently become one of the richest men on the planet? These people had a gift, but more than that, they had powerful principles that set them apart.

I was sure they had some special ability or superhuman powers. As the years went by and I grew to understand what makes a person successful, it occurred to me that life isn't as complicated as we make it out to be.

We don't have to wait to learn a special skill or hope that motivation kicks in. If you are waiting for the day when a genie appears to grant you three wishes, you'll spend your life dreaming and not doing.

Destiny: A Call to Action

The ability to succeed and create the life you really want has always been a choice and not some random event. We are not just actors on a stage reading lines; we can write our lines as we go.

Your destiny is the story of your life, and you get to tell the story your way. Of course, life is full of many variables beyond our control, but at the end of the day, you determine the actions that influence your path.

In this book, I'll show you the key areas you can master to empower your destiny and transform, reinvent, and create anything you want. Nothing is impossible when you apply the thoughts necessary that support your positive mindset.

Your destiny, the course that your life is taking right now, is like a script that has yet to be written. It is being created by you—right now—as you make choices and take intentional action in the form of daily habits and rituals.

How you decide to spend the rest of your days is up to you. It begins with a decision:

Will you **forge a destiny** that is yours, or just let life happen?

SECTION I:
The Force of Destiny

"You are the master of your own destiny. Use your strengths well. They are the keys to your destiny and your success in life. Once you know yourself and take action to realize your dreams, you can unlock the doors to your own potential."

— Neil Somerville

The Master of Decision

"It is in your moments of decision that your
destiny is shaped."

— Tony Robbins

We make thousands of decisions per week: what to
eat, where to go, what clothes to wear, or who to
hang out with on Friday night. As adults, we have to
make critical choices such as which university to attend,
what courses to take, or when to marry and to whom.
These decisions are setting the stage for your life's
destination.

Similar to driving a car down a long highway, you
eventually reach a point in the road and you must decide
whether to turn right or left. How do you know which
decision is the right one? What if you allow fate to
decide?

Channeling the Power of Decision

Decision-making is never easy, but as Tony Robbins
said, "It's in your moments of decision that your destiny
is shaped."

But making a decision is only the first step. You have to
commit to your decision and take deliberate action to
reach the desired outcome.

It is important to ask these critical questions:

- What action would you choose right now if you could
  make one decision?
- What decision, if made, could potentially change
  everything for you?

Don't think about the result or the ultimate outcome; take a moment to make the decision that you've been struggling with the most. Then, focus on the actions that will take you straight to your goal.

Now, a real decision isn't just a lofty wish or a dream. If you say, "I want to earn ten thousand dollars per month doing what I love," that sounds good, but there is nothing here to indicate that you will do that.

We all "want" things. We want to be healthier, earn more money, and spend more time with friends and family. But wanting it and deciding you're going to have it are unrelated. Wishes are for birthdays and shooting stars, but knowing without a doubt what you want and how you're going to get it is a concrete commitment.

You must believe in your decision, too. In the next chapter, we will take a look at the power of our beliefs. For now, just know that believing in this process is a necessary element.

I told you earlier in the introduction that years ago I made a decision to change my life. I decided I would quit my job, do what I wanted, and travel the world, even though I wasn't 100 percent sure what I wanted to do. But I also made another decision that day. I decided what I didn't want.

I didn't want to waste my life fulfilling the expectations of others. I no longer wanted to wake up feeling defeated. I didn't want to feel stuck.

The moment I made this decision, I began piecing together my plan. Did I know how I would do this? Was I ready to leave behind my friends and parents? Was it a wise choice to fly to a country where I didn't speak the language? If I had thought too much about it and weighed the pros and cons, my self-doubt and fear would have swayed my decision. I'd still be doing work I hate, living a menial existence, and wondering, "What might have happened if—?"

That is why I urge you to ground your dream into your subconscious once you make your choice. We don't know the outcome. We can plan for the best, but the rest is up to the small actions you take every day that fortify your decision. Every decision has to be followed by action.

Have you ever said you would do something, but the day never came? Ten years passed and you're still talking about the things you want to do. If this is you, it's time to turn this around.

Those who are unhappy and wishing they had more, or could do more—in many ways, they've decided to live that way. By not deciding, you are deciding. It works both ways.

If you are stuck and blaming your environment, your spouse, or your circumstances for the way life has turned out, you have decided to accept that reality. Our decisions can destroy us, and it is the decisions we don't make that ultimately lead to lives of discontent and unfulfilled dreams.

Everything now rests on your ability to decide what you want. Develop an umbrella plan in which you can envision the plan as a whole. The details come later.

Making a decision can be a great challenge for most people. In many ways, we are accustomed to others making the decisions for us. As children, our parents made decisions for us.

In school, we heard advice and suggestions from teachers and classmates that influenced our decisions. When you need financial help, you visit the bank and talk with someone who couldn't care less about your money, but they'll gladly help you decide where to put it. Then, you get married and your spouse or extended family ends up making decisions that influence your destiny.

Eventually you feel lost, confused, as if your life is no longer your own. This happens when we let others decide our fate. It is a pattern of passive action, or learned helplessness.

According to the Locus of Control concept, individuals with a strong internal locus of control believe the events in their life derive primarily from their own actions. Making core decisions that impact your life is an example of internal control. You decide what you want and you take the actions driving you toward your goals.

Certainly, every decision that is not made by you but by someone else is going to leave you feeling powerless. Sure, you might feel some relief at the time: "Wow, I'm glad she decided that, because I couldn't." However, remember it will come back to you someday if you choose leave your destiny in someone else's hands.

It's perfectly fine to ask people for advice or help, but remember that the decisions you make put you in control of your life. The decisions other people are making takes that control away, even if it works out in your favor.

Most decisions are made out of fear: the fear of making a mistake, the fear of living with a bad outcome. But that is how personal mastery is created.

Yes, fear is the governing force behind your decisions. We are not aware of it but when we fear taking a risk, or think too long on the outcome, it is the fear of making a mistake, of losing the game, that controls the commitment power behind our decision. If a decision is easy, it isn't going to have an impact.

When we surrender our decision-making ability to others, we fall into the trap of being directed by circumstances beyond our control. We end up playing by someone else's rules and we give up the power to make our own. This goes for anything: financial decisions, work, marriage, or other decisions that appear too big to manage.

A standard sailboat has a main sail and a jib. What would happen if you suddenly stopped maneuvering with the large sail? You would likely drift out to sea at the mercy of the ocean's power, or crash into a reef. Even if you tried to maintain control with the smaller sail, the front jib, it wouldn't be enough to direct your boat. You need to be at the helm at all times. You are either the captain of your vessel, or someone else is.

Your destiny can only be measured by the amount of direct influence you put into it. People who go with the flow, failing to take responsibility, and play the victim role of "there's nothing I can do," will end up lost at sea. They may reach land, but it is usually a destination they reached by blind luck. Chances are, many people you know fit this description. They are unhappy, lost, and desperate. Why? They haven't made a decision about where they want to be in life.

You can't get where you want to be if you don't know where that is. It sounds like a simple concept, but many are lost on the journey. They fail to decide what they want, then fail to commit to any course of action.

The Instant Success Myth

Many people want instant success. They are impatient to wait five, ten, or even twenty years for their dreams. We live in a society that can grant us anything right away.

The concept of focus is often lost when we have so much external stimuli capturing our attention day in and day out. Our attention spans are shorter, and so is our tolerance and patience.

Jerry Seinfeld, the well-known creator of the Seinfeld show, is worth $870 million dollars and is perhaps the most successful comedian in show business. But how long did it take him to get there?

Approximately fifteen years. He spent fifteen years on stage, getting thrown off stage, and missing more than he hit. With a lot of hard work and perseverance, anything is possible. But just because it's possible doesn't mean that most people will succeed. Anyone can create the life they want, but if it were easy, everyone would be doing it.

This is the golden ticket. It really is what separates the winners who create a life from the people who end up taking what they can get.

No matter what happens—whether the economy collapses, if you lose your home and end up on the streets, no matter what challenges you're facing right now—you must be 100 percent ready to commit.

You have to burn your ships at the harbor and fight for your life. This may sound overly dramatic, but I know of no other dream that is forged with anything less. If you truly believe in what you stand for, if you really want to create a destiny that is an unforgettable journey, get ready to dig in and charge forward.

If you fall down, you can always get back up. It doesn't matter how many times you get knocked down, either. If you fail, you can try again, and keep pushing ahead.

The only failure in life is staying down and giving up. You can only be defeated when you decide that the game is over.

The Pivotal Moment

"The prison of the past is one you must escape in order to pivot. Our job now is to find out where your attachments to the past lie."

— **Adam Markel**, author of *Pivot: The Art and Science of Reinventing Your Career and Life*

For those who are successful, it all comes down to a moment in their life during which they made a decision to do something that would set in motion the events that shaped their lives.

This is the **Pivotal Moment**.

Can you name the one defining moment in your life in which you turned your destiny into a course of action? What was the decision you made that sent you in the direction you most desired?

If you haven't had a defining moment yet, don't worry. You can now become mindful of the moment when it presents itself. The moment of your greatest fear, when you have to decide whether or not to take action, could be the moment that changes everything.

Your pivotal moment is the instant you realize precisely what you want to do with your life. You might decide to start your own business, join a triathlon, quit your dead-end job and do what you love, move to another city to start a new life, or choose to develop a new habit that creates a different set of actions.

Your moment of realization is the pivotal turn that can fuel your purpose through those moments of doubt, fear, and uncertainty. It will reinforce your decision, injecting courage whenever you second-guess yourself.

Pivotal Moments in History

Rosa Parks made a pivotal decision on the day she decided to refuse to give up her seat to a white passenger on a segregated bus in Alabama.

J.K. Rowling made a pivotal decision when she decided to rise up from her failure and rebuild her life, thus creating a series of bestselling books that sold over four hundred million copies and made her a billionaire.

Bill Gates made a pivotal decision the moment he decided to contact a growing company called MITS (Micro Instrumentation and Telemetry Systems) to negotiate a deal for a BASIC interpreter for their Altair 8800 system. But at the time of setting up this meeting, he and co-founder Paul Allen hadn't even created the code yet.

Arnold Schwarzenegger made a pivotal decision when he decided to sneak out of the barracks of the Austrian military where he was serving two years compulsory service. The reason: To participate in the Mr. Europe bodybuilding competition in Germany, which he won, thereby setting his bodybuilding career in motion.

Viktor E. Frankl, who spent three years in various concentration camps until he was liberated in 1945, made his pivotal moment daily by choosing not to be defeated by the powers that threatened to take away his freedom. Frankl became aware that each of us has the power to define our lives by the choices we make and how to respond to circumstances instead of being made a victim by them.

Colonel Harland David Sanders made a pivotal decision in 1956 when a new interstate bypassed his restaurant, putting him out of business and leaving him with a monthly security check of $105. He decided he wouldn't settle for a quiet retirement, and after packing up his car with two pressure cookers, he hit the road, traveling from restaurant to restaurant selling his recipe.

The Difference Between a Challenge and Impossibility

There are two types of people I come across: those who are challenged by a new idea, and those who think it's impossible.

To live the life you want, you have to believe in what is possible, even if it doesn't feel realistic.

For example, you might set a goal for yourself to double your income in six months. Now, this might seem like a difficult goal to achieve. After all, you work for a company that pays you a set amount each month. You just got a raise at the end of your contract and so there won't be additional income from this company in the foreseeable future. Therefore, if you only rely on this income, the goal becomes impossible. So, how do you get around this and double your income?

You could create a side hustle that brings in additional income. This is where the impossibility becomes a challenge. We know it's possible to make more money, but it's very difficult if you are relying on just one income stream that you can't control. You need an additional source, or perhaps two.

By looking outside the box, you are opening your imagination to greater possibilities. It may take you longer than six months to double your income, but if you create a plan, take action, and stay consistent in your habits, you could achieve your goal.

If you tell most people they could earn a million dollars in the next year, they will tell you it's impossible. They're right—because if you're only making $87,000 a year at one job, you won't be earning a million bucks if things remain the same.

When you begin thinking about how you can make this happen, you're thinking like a challenger. How can I earn that much money on the side? How hard would I have to work to set up a system that would generate this much income? Why do I believe this is impossible?

Life is full of challenges and impossibilities. It is impossible for you to move a heavy object if you just push it with your hands. But give yourself enough leverage, and anything becomes possible. We need this leverage in our lives to move heavy obstacles that are in the way so we can do greater things.

Your **pivotal decision** is that leverage.

Those who have accepted their situation as it is are making excuses, stuck because they refuse to see other possibilities. When we believe that a goal is impossible, it will remain that way until somebody else proves it can be done. Why wait for someone to prove it to you when you can make your dreams a reality?

As long as you stay committed to moving beyond your comfort zone, you will be driven to think outside the box. This is where our unique and creative ideas are born.

We can train ourselves to push our desires to want more than we have been given, and to crave that sense of freedom that belongs to you the moment you claim it. All you need is the resilience to say yes, and the commitment to put your plan into forward motion.

A destiny is created when we take action and push our fears out of the way.

A baby can't walk, eat on its own, or figure out complex problems. But give that baby time to grow and he or she will be capable of anything. With the proper guidance, love, and encouragement, there is nothing a child can't one day accomplish.

The same is true for anyone. We have forgotten what it's like to be a child, to dream, to not let fear defeat us. If fear is defeating you, remember you were once unafraid of the world. You can become that fearless warrior again.

Make your pivotal decision. Let go of the outcome. Engage in fearless confidence.

Action Tasks

- What was the pivotal moment that changed your life? If you haven't had one yet, what would you like it to be?
- What decision are you putting off right now?
- What opportunity are you holding back on pursuing?
- How do you visualize the course of your life after one year? Two years? Five or ten?

In the next chapter, let's talk more about the **power of beliefs** and how they can shape our lives.

Beliefs: The Ultimate Destiny Makers

"It's the repetition of affirmations that leads to belief. And once that belief becomes a deep conviction, things begin to happen."

— Muhammad Ali

A belief is a deeply-rooted thought, idea, or conviction that serves as the mainframe for making decisions, conducting our behavior, and managing self-control over our feelings, thoughts, and emotions.

Your core beliefs lead to successes and failures. Your beliefs are like puppeteers, pulling at your strings and causing you to react based on past beliefs and experiences, defining the path for who and what you will become.

A Sense of Absolute Certainty

Beliefs set the standard for everything that is possible in your life. They are the powerful engines of certainty and deep-rooted convictions. If you want to be the force that controls your own destiny, you must learn to control your beliefs. They have the power to build you up or ruin you.

The reality you live in is a reflection of what you believe. If you are happy and prosperous, with a positive outlook and attitude, it is because you are engaging in an empowering belief system that has created this way of life.

Your reinforcement of internal beliefs are either empowering or disempowering the life you are living. Ask yourself: Are your current beliefs setting you up for success? Or are they holding you back from living the life you want?

Beliefs are incredibly persuasive, continuously shaping the course of our lives. You can dictate the beliefs that guide your life. You can choose to believe that good things are happening all around you, or you can choose not to believe in anything and take your chances.

In the moment you realize you are not a victim of circumstances, but the creator of them, your destiny is shaped.

You can manage your destiny through a system of intentional choice, and abandon your dependence on luck. What you believe in is what you take action on.

You can hold on to your old beliefs and get what you have always received, or you can expand your way of thinking, mapping out and creating a new belief system, setting a new criteria for yourself, with empowering dreams and goals that excite and challenge you. Whatever happened in the past does not have to be your future. What you believed in yesterday you can change today.

Powerful beliefs open new doors, make the impossible possible, and give you the energy to go ahead with the construction of your dreams. Negative beliefs, on the other hand, are anchors weighing you down, corrupting your performance and weakening your internal structure.

Your belief is a deep conviction that convinces the subconscious of something that is supposed to be true. This doesn't mean that it is true; it just means that it is true for you. Your beliefs act as filtering stations that sort out our perceptions of the world.

Our belief system is equipped with a unique selection process that filters the information we receive and discards the rest. Once you are introduced to an idea or concept that fits in to your present reality and current needs, the idea is given an evidence test. Your conscious mind will seek evidence to support the belief, and if it's viable, you will act on it.

If you are still uncertain of the impact that empowering beliefs really have, take a look at some of the world's most prominent people and study the beliefs that turned them into super-achievers.

It is the strength of beliefs that created entrepreneurial icons like Henry Ford and Ray Krok; sports heroes Mohammed Ali and Michael Jordan; the creative genius of Leonardo Da Vinci, Johann Wolfgang Von Goethe, and Wolfgang Amadeus Mozart; and the modern day legendary icons Steven Spielberg, J.K. Rowling, and Bill Gates.

All these people succeeded because they believed they could. They had doubts like everyone else, but their beliefs were stronger than the doubts that threatened to hold them back. Once you create an unbreakable foundation of certainty and channel it into your belief system, you become unbreakable.

Within the belief systems of these icons, there is an unshakable, all-empowering confidence that has been at work from the very beginning. They were not born with it; they created it with strong support from their mentors and coaches, and their own inner drive to succeed where others would fail.

If a trek of one thousand miles begins with the first step, that first step must be a step of faith. Empowering beliefs create powerful outcomes. Our beliefs shape the world we live in and determine the course of action. What you believed in yesterday doesn't have to be the same thing you believe in today.

Beliefs that hold on to the past are dragging you down. It's important to understand the basic steps behind how a belief is created.

Changing Your Beliefs

I want you to think about this quote for a moment by Napoleon Hill:

> "Whatever the mind can conceive and believe, it can achieve."

If this quote is true, and we believe it, then our beliefs have massive influence on our destiny. But even better than that, beliefs are not set in stone. We can change them if we apply a specific process. When our beliefs fail us, it's time to take action and think, behave, and believe differently.

You are responsible for the beliefs you choose to create. Regardless of what you have been taught, you are in control of your own state of mind. With the right tools and guidance, there is nothing in your life that cannot be created or reinvented. Now, let's take a look at making some changes in our belief system.

You should consider changing your beliefs if they:

- No longer support your current goals, dreams, and mission.
- Feed into and supports negative thoughts and destructive behavior.
- Limit your potential for success.
- Prevent you from taking action toward the fulfillment of your great purpose.

We can all make changes in regard to our beliefs. Some of these beliefs are easy to spot, resting in plain sight on the surface. Others are less obvious and require a deeper level of insight and acute awareness. As you work on altering these beliefs, you will start to notice changes in your own physiology.

Emotionally, you will start to feel better about who you are. Physically, you will feel stronger and look better. Mentally, you will be more focused on your needs, as well as on the needs of others.

Change Your Limiting Beliefs: The Six-Step Process

Believe it or not, you can change a belief in an instant. The challenge is in recognizing the beliefs that should be switched so they are in alignment with your current values and needs.

It is important to understand that beliefs have created the circumstances in our lives. When we change something, we can change the circumstances. This is one way to experience a transformation. In almost every case, this requires the following changes:

1. An individual must change their beliefs about something.
2. And they must change the thoughts supporting those beliefs.

Here are six steps you can take to begin changing anything in your life. Keep in mind that this takes time and you won't always succeed by doing something once or twice. Like any habit, you have to keep at it.

Step 1: Identify the belief you want to change.
This is the first step to taking positive action. You can only change something if you know what you need to change, and why you want to change it.

Core negative beliefs that make you feel inferior, inadequate, or worthless should be first on your list. Why hang on to your painful thoughts any longer? This is a tough step for most people. We have been feeding into our pain for so long it starts to appear normal.

I can assure you that in working through your pain, and recognizing the negative beliefs you created about yourself, your life will begin to take a dramatic shift.

Here are some examples of beliefs you may have about yourself. See if you recognize any of these:

"Everything bad that happens to me is my fault."

"I feel like I am less competent than everyone else when it comes to success or getting ahead in life."

"I feel like a failure or a 'nobody' when in the presence of other people who are obviously better than me."

"I have no qualities worth talking about that anyone would be interested in."

"I should be perfect at all times. I have to show people I am perfect."

"I am inherently flawed."

"I am inferior. Everyone else is smarter, more educated, and they seem to land on their feet when all I do is fail from day to day."

"I'm no good, and everyone knows it."

"Once someone gets to know me, they will just leave me like everyone else."

"My family was extremely dysfunctional; so, I am dysfunctional."

"If only she would stop treating me that way, I'd feel better about this situation and myself."

You might have a number of faulty beliefs about yourself that have disempowered you throughout most of your life. I know I did before I worked to turn them around. The key is to recognize what they are. Some are buried deep. Others are more noticeable and are running through your mind a hundred times a day. They feel so normal that you don't question their validity.

Take time to write them out and list as many as you can. You can start with parts of the short list above that apply and add to it with your own negative beliefs. Pay attention to the beliefs that target your self-esteem and devalue your worth.

Step 2: Disempower the old belief by injecting doubt and uncertainty. It is time to take a stand and question your belief thoroughly, analyzing it under a mental microscope through strict analysis. It is time to put your beliefs on trial.

You are going to question your beliefs, attack their vulnerability, tear down their walls, and weaken their structure. If a belief has been built on lies and falsehoods, it will not stand up to the scrutiny of your attack.

Here is an example:

"My family was extremely dysfunctional; so, I am dysfunctional."

Begin by questioning this belief. Take away its power. Make a decision to reject it. Here's what I wrote.

"What is the basis for this belief?"

"My family life was not perfect by any means. My parents loved me conditionally and they had their own issues to deal with. Many times I felt rejected. But this doesn't mean I am dysfunctional. To a degree, isn't everyone? Don't we all struggle with our own defects? I refuse to accept this belief anymore."

Go deep with your ideas and push back hard. Then, ask pertinent questions that disengage the power your belief has over you. Put your belief on trial! Tell yourself that this is not a reality you choose to believe in anymore. Disown it completely. Choose to believe in something else. This is when your mind makes a shift toward reframing what it has been trained to accept.

Step 3: Reframe the new belief while discarding the old one. Full of fear, self-doubt, and lacking confidence, we can easily slip back into old patterns of defeat. We can convince ourselves that negative beliefs are true.

When you decide to replace your old beliefs, you are making a firm commitment: I refuse to feel this way anymore. From now on, I am going to reject all negative thoughts. If you do this enough, you will be thinking and behaving differently.

Step 4: Visualize the person you will become once you have created a new belief. Visualize yourself behaving differently, taking new and decisive actions, and pushing through your fear instead of being blocked by it. See yourself overcoming the obstacles that, until now, have been holding you back. Imagine the new way of life that waits for you on the other side of conquering your fears.

Then, visualize the steps that you would need to take to make this transition. What could you do right now to begin building momentum? How would you have to think and act to achieve an outcome that is seemingly beyond your reach or capability? Once you have the clear answer, it is time to start being that person.

Step 5: Reinforce the new belief, taking further repetitive action toward making it real. Now that you have a solid idea of the changes you want, start by supporting your new belief. Take immediate action and reframe your old belief with the new one.

If you tear down the old belief but do nothing to replace it, you'll eventually resort to that old destructive way of thinking. When this happens, just remember what your replacement belief is and continue to reinforce it over and over. Such reinforcement has to be done consistently in order to succeed.

Try writing out ten of your favorite quotes. Utilize the power of positive words and affirmations. Repeat these several times a day. It will be uncomfortable at first, but be persistent.

The more you use words of positive power, the faster you can shift your beliefs to accepting what you are saying and thinking. Persistence and consistency are the keys. Soon you will be able to pull out your positive mental toolbox and use it to overpower negative thoughts and words.

Self-conversation is a powerful tool. Your negative beliefs used this tool against you for many years. Now you know that you can choose thoughts that support your new belief. Give your new belief lots of encouragement and support. Repeat it as many times as you need to. Convince yourself that it is true!

Step 6: Follow-up with action. In this final stage, you are going to continually strengthen your belief through convincing evidence. You will alter your actions and behaviors to align with the new belief as it starts planting roots deep in your subconscious.

It is important to reinforce the new beliefs on a continual basis. Create the beliefs you want to have. Do not settle on thoughts that devalue you.

Once a year, you could give yourself a small test to see where you are with your beliefs, and analyze whether they are consistent with your desires and purpose.

You may discover, as I have, that there are new discrepancies with your current beliefs and values. If so, you can always update your belief system every year, making subtle changes here and there, adjusting your course in order to stay on track.

Six Beliefs of Self-Empowerment

Beliefs construct the foundation upon which our lives are built. In structuring and reconstructing these beliefs to match the life we seek to govern, there are six areas we should focus our energy on.

Believe in Yourself

Personal excellence begins with a belief in yourself, in your abilities, and in your talents. Believe without a doubt that you can, and you will; believe that you can't, and the opposite holds true. Your level of genuine belief in yourself determines the experiences you will have and the level of successful choices you make.

Self-doubt leads to poor choices; these choices lead to painful outcomes and poor results, poor job situations, and choosing friends and partners who are not supportive or compatible.

A powerful belief system begins with the fundamental basics of believing in who you are and a sense of knowing that you are going to make it no matter what, and that everything you desire is being drawn to you right now. A firm belief in something—an idea, a thought, or principle—is a magnet that attracts the opportunity and the right people at just the right time to make it all happen.

Beliefs act as filters that determine our perceptions of the world, and it is through these perceptions that beliefs are structured and formed.

Believing in yourself is an inside job. It is accepting yourself just as you are today. Believe that you can do anything you truly commit to, because you can. When we choose to believe in the possibilities, we bring what is possible into the real world. In other words, we make it happen. Don't waste another minute of your time stuck on the failures of the past when you should be focusing on today and what you can do.

Believe in Children

Children have many important requirements that need to be fulfilled so they can grow and develop into strong, confident adults. The foundation for success in a person's life begins at a very young age, when they start to absorb the energy that makes up their learning environment and surroundings.

As part of this environment, children are exposed to an entire world of various beliefs and ideas and, without really knowing why, they simulate the beliefs that eventually shape the course of their lives.

As parents, teachers, and the guardians of our children, we have a responsibility to teach, guide, and listen, to show them the right way to self-expression, love, and instruction.

It is the true nature of a child to trust people, especially adults, and it's the responsibility of parents, big brothers and sisters, role models, and teachers to encourage trust through genuine encouragement and praise. What children hear, see, and value are internalized into core beliefs and can transform the direction of their lives.

If you show a child you believe in them and give them the support they need by providing assurance that they're loved and appreciated, the child will grow up with powerful social tools to handle the fear of the world and develop high confidence and self-esteem.

An environment that instills fear of failure and lacks support or appreciation eventually fails the child, and the beliefs they internalize can erupt into self-destructive habits. This can be prevented if childhood lessons are set right.

Think about your own childhood and recall the people who changed your life with just a single word or kind gesture. What beliefs did you internalize due to the influence of others? What beliefs did you realize were damaging to you?

Model the Beliefs of Successful People

You can emulate the success of your mentors if you study the system of beliefs they used as a pathway toward personal excellence.

Do you want to build financial freedom? Would you like to lose weight? Run a marathon? Build the perfect career? Anything is possible when you follow the beliefs of those who've already achieved what you desire.

To be the person you want to become, start spending time with those who live the way you want to. Emulate their actions and behaviors, but—most importantly—model their beliefs and make them your own. Successful people who accomplish great things in their lifetime have superior belief systems—beliefs that stretch to the unlimited pathways of excellence.

Believe in Your Dream and Life Mission

When you believe in your life purpose, it provides you with the focus and confidence to make clearer decisions as to the direction you need to take to fulfill your mission. Believing in a powerful destiny means believing in something bigger than yourself. One of the best techniques for solidifying belief in your dream is by reciting a daily mantra. Here's an example of just one mantra that I often repeat to myself:

> *"I have a purpose and a destiny, and it is unfolding right now! I am doing great things with my life and I will continue to do great things as long as I stay true to who I am and the person I want to become. I believe I am becoming that great person right now! As I construct the roads for the future, planting the seeds of my soul in rich places to grow, my mission and destiny is attracting everything I need for today."*

Create a powerful mantra or a list of your favorite affirmations and repeat them to yourself every day to reaffirm your beliefs in what you're doing and the path unfolding before you. Make this a daily habit, and you will attract the people and situations that are necessary for the unfolding pathways of your life.

Remember, believing in your dream means taking action. You can't just believe and hope that it works out. Believers are doers. Our actions are fueled by the beliefs that we'll succeed no matter what.

Maybe we don't know how this will happen, but we know that if we persevere, leaving doubt and uncertainty behind, we will find a way. Each day, you must take steps to construct your dream.

Believe in Something Greater Than Yourself

All great achievers believe strongly in what they can do. Through working hard and maintaining absolute focus, a high achiever brings what they desire to fruition.

When you believe in the success that is taking place in your life today, you stop believing in the limitations that prevent you from moving ahead. You trust that success is coming your way.

Successful people are thankful beforehand for the success they have and will continue to have. They are the true believers! I have found that one of the best ways to encourage and strengthen my own beliefs is to help another to strengthen theirs.

Most people fail because they believe in the wrong ideas. They see success as something that exists "out there" and happens to other people, but not to them. They don't believe in success because they have never had it or have never recognized it.

Over the years, the meaning of success has become very misconstrued and our perception about it has altered. It isn't about having the greatest body, the most money or popularity, or even worldwide fame. It can be these things, but it isn't limited to them.

Success is also about friendships, family, and spending long days at the beach or taking walks in the park. The everyday activities of living provide us with the true meaning of success.

Believe that you're succeeding right now, even if you are in a grim state or a moment of suffering. These moments also symbolize the stepping stones to something greater. Once you define what it means to be successful, you'll be in a much better position to create the beliefs you need to accomplish everything you've ever desired.

The Power of "I Can"

When I was a kid, one of my favorite stories was *The Little Engine That Could* by Platt and Munk. It's the perfect story for teaching people about the power of stating "I can." Too often, we carry around the belief that we can't accomplish something or that it's just not possible.

The words you tell yourself have power over your internal strength and convictions. By saying that you can't, you are preventing yourself from learning new skills, solving problems, or moving forward. It would be in your best interest to consider it carefully before responding with, "I can't."

These thoughts cement our limitations, and define our level of success. Imagine you're at the end of your life: How would you feel if you realized that "I can't" was a lie you'd told yourself to escape your fear of acting on your dreams?

Like *The Little Engine That Could*, we must encourage ourselves as well as others. We have to believe in what we can truly accomplish.

When we tell ourselves that we can do it, this feeds in to the empowering belief that anything can happen if we believe it can. You build the mindset of a winner that becomes unstoppable. Most of the wins we achieve in our lifetime has little to do with talent or skill.

It is the ability to create a vision for the life you truly desire. Then, following through with a set action plan to turn that vision into a reality.

SECTION II:
Create a Vision For Your Life

"Imagination is the beginning of creation. You imagine what you desire; you will what you imagine; and at last you create what you will."

— George Bernard Shaw

The Self-Powered Imagination

"I am enough of an artist to draw freely upon my imagination. Imagination is more important than knowledge. Knowledge is limited. Imagination encircles the world."

— Albert Einstein

Everything is created through the universe of your imagination. It is within this imaginative structure that great ideas are realized, artistic concepts developed, and creative thoughts conceived; it is here that the words of poets and literary prophets are expressed, and scientific theories become real possibilities leading to breakthroughs.

The visual imagination stretches beyond the limited boundaries of basic two-dimensional thought. It reveals how a treasure chest of mental images can change the world we live in almost instantly.

Visualization is a creative machine that brings limitless opportunity for advancement in science, the arts, technology, and spiritual progress. It is also used to achieve the most impossible of goals. People from varying backgrounds, education, cultures, and social levels around the world have learned to master the art of visual imagination to attain wealth, freedom, creativity, and expression.

The power of the imagination is the beginning stage of all creation. Nothing happens unless it is first designed as a visual form within the mind. Everything you are going to attain and experience in life is designed and then built according to a series of visual images.

It is proven in scientific experiments and deep research that athletes training for the Olympics prepare for the sport both on the field and off. In fact, according to researchers Ellen Rogin and Lisa Kueng, it's not only the physical training that impacts an athlete's success, but the mental training, too. The athletes who commit to visualizing the training, to mentally see themselves succeeding, have the greater chance at winning.

This has been proven by Russian scientists who conducted experiments on the training methods of four groups of athletes:

- Group one: 100% physical training
- Group two: 75% physical training, 25% mental training
- Group three: 50% physical training, 50% mental training
- Group four: 25% physical training, 75% mental training

The fourth group had the best results overall, outperforming the competition in the Olympics.

First, establish a goal. Then, visualize achieving that goal in detail, and stay focused on it over the long-term.

During the Olympics, athletes would use both internal and external visualization. For example, Alpine Skier Lindsay Vonn used her hands to simulate the path of the course through her own eyes. She would visualize herself speeding down the slopes as if she were actually performing in the race.

With external imagery, athletes will visualize themselves competing as if watching it happen from a spectator's view. By implementing this visual imagery using both internal and external visualization, world class athletes could achieve their dreams and improve their performance.

Now, what could you do if you committed to just ten minutes a day of visualization? What goals could you achieve?

To create the destiny you want, you must form a direct link with your imagination. When you treat your thoughts as real things that carry energy, you can train your mind to direct your thoughts into seeing the possibilities. I am a firm believer that goals achieved build dreams, but this happens much quicker if you can visualize the actionable steps to accomplishing your goals.

Visualization keeps you focused as you develop a clear line of concentration. Your imagination is always seeing, planning, and putting together the pieces of your dreams to create what you want. When you focus on a specific goal, you are directing all your mental energy toward an objective that becomes the vision of what you want.

In visualizing your success, you are creating a framework to build upon. A life is measured by the amount of visual planning that supersedes it—not necessarily by the amount of work put into achieving a goal.

When you can visualize your next move, your mind will find a way to make it happen. This could result in a chance encounter with the right person, or in a business proposition that suddenly presents itself.

Visual Architecture — Pathways to a Richer Life

"Visualize this thing you want. See it, feel it, believe in it. Make your mental blueprint and begin."

— Robert Collier

Visual imagination is the creative engine that builds new ventures. It takes an old idea, refines it, polishes it, and perfects it. It turns small businesses into Fortune 500 companies, and converts a good idea into an amazing one. Those who seek to build on this creative mental power have the potential to amass fortunes beyond their wildest dreams.

By integrating the tool of visualization in your daily habits, you develop the capability to become rich in every way. You are the visual architect supplying the plans and blueprints. You bring your ideas to the table; the visual imagination is the carpenter of your dreams.

Destiny Builder: A Short Exercise

Take some time to answer the questions below. This will provide energy to trigger your ideas, and kick-start your imagination into taking action. As you work through the material in this section, take time each day to sit down and think about what matters most to you.

- What would you do if there were no limitations to the kind of life you desire?

- How would you spend the rest of your days if you could do absolutely anything with your time?
- What would it take for you accomplish everything you have ever dreamed possible?
- What would make you the happiest person alive?
- What are the opportunities available to you right now?
- What is stopping you from taking advantage of these opportunities?
- What opportunities do you wish you had? How will you create these opportunities?
- What event do you envision that will have a profound impact on your life?
- What earth-changing events do you visualize taking place in the world in the next fifty years?
- What is the life you visualize living someday?
- What actions could you take every day to bring you closer to achieving this dream?

This is the power of your mental construct. Use it consistently. The more you apply it and with greater frequency and consistency, the stronger your vision of the world you desire to live in becomes a reality.

Applying the Creative Force of Intentional Visualization

What is the kind of life you see yourself living in five years? Do you want to live in a new home in the mountains or by the sea? Take an adventurous trip around the world? Visit exotic locations or trek through the mountains of Nepal? How about scuba diving for old wrecks in Palau or Bali? Do you visualize yourself becoming a successful business entrepreneur? How about a published author? Could you be the next researcher who discovers a new cure?

Do you visualize meeting the partner of your dreams? Becoming a powerful public speaker or presenter? Do you envision yourself as a great leader with the ability to change the course of a nation's future? Creating a new product that helps people improve their quality of life?

Once you put your creative imagination to work, visual imagery begins to form.

The source of your greatest power is not something you have to obtain; you already have all the tools you need. What you have been lacking is not knowledge or skill but a **vision for the life** you want to be leading.

Too many people have forgotten how to dream. They become 'educated' and brainwashed into thinking dreams are for kids. When we get to a certain stage in life, we are told to stop dreaming and start thinking realistically about the future. Where is this reality? Who is creating it? Why do we have to rely on someone else to give us the life we want?

As long as you allow the world to run the show for you, your destiny will always be in the hands of someone else. Your choices will be made for you, and you will become dependent on a system that will eventually fail you. Life fails those who give up on their dreams to follow someone else's plan.

By tapping into the creativity of your unlimited imagination, the forces of the universe are triggered and immediately go to work to grant you all the things you can imagine, and much more.

I have heard many people say, "I have no imagination. I am not creative at all. I can't draw, paint, or build anything!" Well, all of this might be true, except for the part about having no imagination. In most cases, it isn't a lack of money, resources, or limited time that makes us fail—it is a lack of vision.

More people fail because of a lack of creative imagination. Unfortunately, those same people who think this way also live desperate lives of futility, never having accomplished their true dreams or attaining a level of success they feel comfortable with.

In the end, what matters is that you're working toward something you feel good about. You don't have to be a Warren Buffet, Steve Jobs, or Bill Gates to be considered successful. You just have to be you, and the success you feel is congruent with the principles you hold at great value.

Let your imagination run wild with all the things you've always imagined doing. Let go of the idea that you have to be realistic about what is possible; this is where our limitations exist. If you want a life that makes a difference, you have to become unconventional in your approach.

Free your visual artistry to explore, expand, and grow. Let your mind operate without restraint, without boundaries. You have to "see" the world you wish to live in. The first step is to see what you want, then take the necessary actions to get there. When we can envision the life we want, the actions we need to take to move toward those goals are much clearer.

Visualizing the life you intend to lead is setting up all future actions to pivot toward making it happen. You are not just visualizing what you want to achieve, but how you are going to get there.

Visionary Architects

For centuries, people have been applying their imagination to create artistic visions of their lifelong dreams and goals. These master visionaries—from Confucius to Thomas Edison and Steve Jobs—have discovered again and again that what you visualize through imagination has a high probability of coming true.

Since the early days of ancient Greek philosophers and writers, the master visionaries have been telling us, "See what you want to achieve, imagine it as having already happened, and it will be yours."

Visualizing the experiences you want to have is a concept that has been taught from the beginning. It still applies today in observing the success of world leaders, entertainers, and world class business moguls who have demonstrated what is possible when you have a purpose supported by vision, and the vision is supported by solid goals and strong beliefs.

Jim Henson, the famous puppeteer who changed the world of entertainment, applied his creative imagination to entertaining millions of people around the world with his unforgettable characters that appeared in both The Muppets and Sesame Street. Jim Henson, with his artistic imagination, could visualize the potential of television puppetry and pioneered great advances as a result.

Henson's imagination gave life, emotion, and voices to some of the most well-known characters on television and in movies. His legacy is still alive today as millions of children (and adults) are entertained and educated through the visual concepts Henson began creating over fifty years ago.

Ray Kroc, a leader in the entrepreneurial business, visualized McDonald's restaurants lined up and down every street in America. He applied a high-powered imagination to fulfilling his dreams. McDonald's is now the largest hamburger fast food restaurant in the world, with over 31,000 stores worldwide serving tens of millions of people daily.

Legendary filmmaker **Steven Spielberg**, when creating such blockbusters as Raiders of the Lost Ark and Close Encounters of the Third Kind, would visualize every scene frame by frame, and by utilizing the creative talent of visual artists, sketch out each scene step by step.

Through a visionary technique called storyboarding, filmmakers such as Spielberg were able to create each scene as it would appear in the film, adding greater depth and detail. Spielberg's visual imagination has been shared with millions of people around the world for over forty years.

Walt Disney, the great American film producer and entertainer, visualized building the greatest theme park in the world. Although he died before its completion, his vision lived on in the minds of those closest to him, who completed what is known as Walt Disney World. Today, Walt Disney World Resort is the world's largest and most frequented entertainment resort in the world, with millions of visitors each year.

Henry Ford, founder of the Ford Motor Company, created a global vision that changed the world. He dreamed of a world in which consumerism was the key to peace, and this led to the mass production of inexpensive goods and high wages for workers.

His innovations led to the introduction of the assembly line, which enabled products to be mass-produced at reduced costs, designing a way of life in which the average middle-class American could afford an automobile, making him one of the richest and most powerful men in the world. Henry Ford's visual acuity revolutionized the automobile industry and gave rise to a new era of growth and prosperity.

Thomas Edison—an American inventor, researcher, scientist, and businessman—became one of the world's most prolific visionaries, with 1,093 patents in his name.

The inventor of the motion picture camera and the light bulb, Thomas Edison changed the world when he brought his vision to life with the implementation of electric power generation and distribution networks to factories, businesses, and homes.

Steve Jobs, co-founder and CEO of Apple Inc., was one of the greatest visionaries of the 21st century. Jobs possessed a magnificent visionary talent that allowed him to see the future potential of an idea, concept, or existing invention years ahead of competition.

Jobs' creative genius and unique design sense led to the development of a wide range of high-level computer and portable electronic device technologies that continue to change the way people communicate and do business every day.

Gandhi freed a nation from British rule, and he manifested his goals with nothing more than a belief.

The imagination and visual creativity that worked for these world-class achievers is the same available to anyone. Visualization works for all of us. You only have to have the willingness to open up your mind to the unlimited potential available to you. Your imagination is the tool that can turn your vision into a reality.

The masters who have achieved personal success envisioned the world they wanted to create until there was no doubt within their conscious—and subconscious—minds that this was what they had to have.

The success of an individual begins with an idea, the idea grows into a possibility, and the possibility becomes a vision. The vision becomes a goal, and the goal, once a specific course of action is applied, is achieved to produce a set of desired results. This is the power of visual blueprinting.

Creating Your Visual Roadmap

"The only thing worse than being blind is having sight and no vision."

— Helen Keller

If you fail to create the vision of where you want to be and what you want to do and have, you will end up in a place you don't really want to be, doing something you never wanted to do, stuck with the things you never desired in the first place.

You need a vision of where you are going. This visual roadmap is your guide for getting where you want to go. Without a clear map to follow, all roads will lead to dead ends.

Without a vision of what you want, you will always be at the mercy of circumstances created by others. But having formed a plan, you can be confident that the road you are on is the right one. Every great success story began with an idea, a vision, and a plan of action that consists of concrete steps.

When visualizing, follow these steps:

1. Decide what do you want to be, do, and have.

If you know exactly what you want, you can focus on obtaining it. Once you have made the decision and committed all your resources and energy to going after your dreams with a relentless passion, nothing can stop you. Concentrate on whatever fills you with excitement and keeps you awake late at night, thinking, "This is what I want! I must have it!"

Set aside twenty minutes in the morning and evening for this exercise. Sit quietly and imagine the life you are leading. What work are you doing? Where are you living? Who are you with? Where do you want to be a year from now? See yourself doing the work you love, spending time with people you care about. Make your vision as vivid as you can.

Make a firm decision about what you want to be, do, and have. By making a commitment to your new way of life, you will be more motivated to channel your energy into the areas that need your attention.

2. Believe in the power of your vision.

Your belief system is a support structure that holds a creative vision in place. It also supports the pillars of your imagination. When you apply the power of belief to your visual imagination, you are laying a foundation for the manifestation of your dreams. When you believe, you can push through any level of doubt and dissolve lack of confidence. Believing in your visions adds vitality to reality.

When you envision your future self, believing in that image is the first step to making it come true. Most people believe in what they can see and touch in the moment, so if it isn't there right in front of you, it isn't there at all. This way of thinking limits your vision and blocks the flow of the imagination.

If at first you don't believe in what you're seeing and visualizing, or if it seems too good to be true, keep working at it. Expand your visionary bubble and continue to push through the limitations of your mind. Tell yourself repeatedly, "I know I can have this. There is always a way, and I will find it." Continue to tell yourself that, no matter how crazy or unrealistic it might appear to be. There's always a way of making it happen.

Believing in your visualizations is the glue that binds the images together to create the world you would like to have. As you trust and have faith in yourself and what you are working for, remember that you will draw to you those things that you believe in the most and can imagine deeply.

The more vivid and detailed the images are, and the stronger you believe in yourself to achieve the impossible, the more driven you will be to work for your goals. A clear vision of where you want to be provides the context for a life that you could have.

3. Align your vision with present values.

Your visions should work together to support your current goals and values. All of this adds a deep and meaningful purpose to your life. Your visual imagery should focus on the values most important to you. If you haven't already done so, make a list of values you will strengthen. Write down these values and commit them to memory.

Then, when you apply your visual imagery to manifesting the person you desire to become, put these values at the very forefront of your imagination. See yourself living these values as if you have already acquired mastery over them. Eventually, without even realizing it, you will have developed and acquired the values that you cherish. Now create the visions that build a solid foundation of self-worth and meaning.

4. Visualize with consistency.

Visualization takes a lot of work before you start to see any results. This isn't just a fast and simple way to get anything you want through wishful thinking and daydreaming; it requires your time and effort in order to grow into something real. Like any tool, it is only as useful as the skill of the one who controls it. The key is to practice this skill on a consistent and regular schedule, and to practice it every day, even if only for ten minutes.

You can do this anytime during the day—when you're on an elevator, in a coffee shop, or standing in line at the supermarket. Use every opportunity to apply your thoughts and build your visions.

If you can't find the time, make the time—even if it's only for five or ten minutes here and there. The secret to mastering any skill is practice. Practice leads to excellence, and excellence leads to self-mastery.

5. Utilize positive affirmations.

An affirmation, or mantra, is a powerful method of convincing the subconscious that a belief or situation already exists.

Through consistently creating and repeating positive statements to yourself, you can turn off the inner rampant dialogue that has been running things and replace it with healthier, more vibrant words of choice that express the emotions and experiences you desire to create. Affirmations follow a set of basic standards, like the ones below:

- An affirmation is always positive and in the present tense.
- Affirmations are short, concise, and to the point.
- An affirmation is personal. It focuses on a belief, value, or principle you desire to integrate into your mental functions.
- An affirmation conveys emotion and feelings.

- Affirmations support your deepest values, and always express the person you are striving to become.

Here are some examples of positive affirmations you can use in your daily life to bring more positive and creative energy into your life.

- Everything in the universe is coming together every day to build purpose in my life.
- I have everything I need within me. My life is overflowing with abundance.
- Everything I visualize happening in my life also desires to be created. It is made real the moment I decide it will happen.

Now, create some of your own affirmations to use every day and enjoy the state of relaxation they bring you.

Techniques for the Visual Artist

"Formulate and stamp indelibly on your mind a mental picture of yourself as succeeding. Hold this picture tenaciously. Never permit it to fade. Your mind will seek to develop the picture."

— Norman Vincent Peale

Applying the process of visual imagination requires steps of action. Here are effective techniques you can apply right away in order to start working these changes into your life.

I would suggest putting aside at least twenty minutes per day. If possible, try to do three sessions at twenty minutes each. Then, focus on a specific technique for at least one week. Take a look at the results and if you think it's working, continue it into the second week. You may have to experiment before settling on your favorite exercise and the one that produces the best results.

The Visual Artist

Drawing, painting, or sketching your visions is an excellent method for producing powerful results, defining your dreams in colors and concise detail. Many people, even if they can't paint or draw very well, favor this method, as it adds depth and significance to goals, enhances dreams, or furthers the advancement of a lifelong career.

Through sketching or painting the images, the mental image of what you desire becomes more life-like and richer in depth with enhanced clarity. A friend of mine whose passion was traveling always sketched pictures of the places she wanted to go, and eventually she found herself on an adventure, visiting those famous sites.

Feel free to sketch, paint, airbrush, or use colored pencils or crayons. On paper or canvas, transfer the image of something you desire to have or experience. This might be a place you want to visit, something you want to experience, or something you wish to attain.

The Image Writer

Using a technique I like to call image writing, you are going to commit to writing two pages a day for thirty days. To get started, buy yourself a clean notebook and go to work. By setting a goal to write two pages a day, you will flush your system by applying to paper anything that's in your mind. Instead of holding your thoughts, ideas, and troubles inside of you, put them on the page.

Image writing is an effective technique for problem solving, brainstorming, and creating and discovering new ideas that you never knew existed. If it weren't for this commitment, I probably never would have gotten around to writing this book, because a lot of the material in these pages came from years of writing down every little idea and thought I had on a daily basis. After several years of doing this, I now have dozens of small notebooks filled with enough material for a dozen more books.

Commit to writing every day for at least one month. Don't take any days off. First, find the best time of day for writing. Is it first thing in the morning, late at night, when everyone else has gone to bed, or during your coffee break in the middle of the day?

Once you have found the most convenient time and a comfortable place, start writing and don't stop. Write continuously until you have emptied your mind completely of the stuff that has been floating around.

Write about the visions you have been having, the dreams you are pursuing, or the obstacles and roadblocks you have to overcome. You can write about anything, because nobody is going to see it except for you.

After thirty days, go back and review the notes you have taken. Is there a pattern to your thoughts and visions? Is there anything you have written that surprises you? After doing this for thirty days, you will have formed a solid habit of writing that is going to help you immensely with controlling and expanding your visions.

If you miss a day, just move your thirty days ahead by one day. Use a calendar and mark off every day that you complete your journal.

The Musical Visionary

Have you ever listened to a song or piece of music and immediately felt compelled to do something? Does music help you visualize and spark your imagination? For most people it does, because music is a powerful medium for visualization. Music stimulates the imagination, and the more you appreciate the music you are listening to, the more stimulated and creative you become.

The type of music you choose to listen to has a powerful effect on your feelings and energy, and can control the direction of your visions. The vision that you want to work on must be supported by the right kind of music, depending, once again, on what it is you want.

Set aside ten minutes each day for this exercise. Now, think about a goal you have, preferably one that is long-term and far out of reach at the moment. Depending on what your goal is, select a piece of music that gets you thinking about it. Have you chosen something loud and with a fast beat or tempo, or something soft, intense, and emotional?

I listen to music every day, and at certain times of the day, I select themes that stir my imagination into action. Be sure that the music you choose is in line with the vision you desire to build. Music is great for creating an atmosphere of emotion for your visual imagination.

Positive Affirmation Session

An affirmation is a form of internal reprogramming designed to erase or record over the internal recordings you have been listening to unconsciously for most of your life. Some examples of affirmations are:

- I can handle any difficult situation with serenity and confidence, seeking the best solution that is fair and just.

- My life is in the right place and I am where I need to be to learn, grow, and make the progress necessary for the advancement of my destiny.

- There isn't any difficulty or situation that I cannot handle, no problem is too big, and as long as I stay positive and in the now, I trust I will do the right thing.

- I lack for nothing. I have all that I need to be happy and I am completely satisfied.

- I am an honest, confident, capable person with compassion for all things.

- I am the master of my destiny, the creator of my world.

- All difficult people and situations are there to make me a stronger and better person.

Create a list of affirmations

Start to compile a master list of affirmations by writing down positive statements about yourself, your life and about other people. Add one new affirmation to this list every day.

Eventually you may have a list of well over a thousand affirmations. That is a lot of positive reprogramming! I suggest ending each of your sessions by repeating, either verbally or mentally, several of these affirmations. Believe the words of power you are speaking and feel the emotional strength behind them.

Forty-Five Minute Power Tri-Combo

Now that we have taken a look at some of the techniques and exercises associated with practicing daily visualization techniques, it is time to review a short program that I call the Forty-Five Minute Power Tri-Combo.

How it works is simple, but for it to be truly effective, you have to practice it at least three times a week. Using the visual exercises suggested, you are going to put together a short daily program that includes doing three of these activities for fifteen minutes.

Suggested Program

Set aside forty-five minutes of the day. Now, for the next forty-five minutes, you are going to perform three of the above exercises in consecutive order, without taking a break. Here is what my program might look like:

1. **The image-writing technique:** For fifteen minutes, I write down any thoughts, ideas, or images that come to mind. This is great for flushing out your

thoughts and paving the way for the next exercise. Only write for fifteen minutes and then begin the next exercise.

2. **The visual meditation exercise:** Do this exercise as described in this chapter. Choose a situation or event you see yourself in and apply your visual images to create the experience. Can you visualize where you will be in ten years, what you will be doing, and the person you will have developed into? Are you retired, or have you changed careers? Are you living the life you have always imagined? See it, feel it, believe it—and then live it.

3. **The musical visionary:** I like to end my session with a piece of music that fits my vision. This could be a classical piece or a song that inspires you. You might want to choose the song before you start your session, or you can spend a couple minutes searching for it right after your mediation is finished.

Another alternative is to play a piece of music while you are performing visual meditation. This often helps to form stronger images during the visual meditation process. If you do these two together, as some people like to do, you should consider this one activity. You will still have to finish off your tri-combo with one more activity, either sketching/painting/coloring or some other creative activity related to your vision.

You can try different combinations and mix up the order of the exercises. Some days you might decide to do only two exercises for twenty minutes each and that is perfectly fine—whatever works for you on that particular day.

Try this at least three times a week if you can't do it every day. Make this one of your greatest habits. It could become the most important forty-five minutes of your day.

Optimum Visualization

Optimum visualization is a very powerful and effective technique. How it works is simple, but applying it to create results is challenging. This is what I refer to as the fast track method for achieving results with the highest rate of efficiency. What it requires is absolute concentration and dedication of all your mental resources.

How it Works

Begin by imagining something you want to achieve. It can be a goal, a project you want to start or complete. Whatever it may be, think about it right now. Think of nothing else but this one thing that you desire to accomplish.

Imagine the actions you need to take in order to have this one thing. Think about those actions and visualize them as you would the rungs on a ladder. See yourself climbing this ladder, and every rung you climb is another action that takes you closer to your goal.

Concentrate and focus on your goal for ten minutes. You can start with a short session and work your way up from there. Think about nothing else except for this one thing. Treat it as if it is everything, as if it is your life's work. If you suddenly find yourself thinking about something else, just let it happen. Acknowledge that another completely unrelated thought has entered your space and then let it go. You can invite it back in later, but for now, just think about what you want to manifest.

By focusing on this and thinking of nothing else but what you want to create, you are directing all your present mental forces into this visual creation and feeding the imagination with a stream of positive energy. This is a form of **laser-focused concentration** that has massive potential to turn a dream into reality when directed with purpose.

Next, believe that your vision has been created. See yourself as existing with this reality as if you have succeeded. If it's a new house, what do you see inside?

If it's a trip around the globe, where do you see yourself journeying? If it's a top position in the company of your choice, how do you imagine your ideal workday? Take in all the details. Fill your mind with the good stuff and paint the picture as big and bright and real as you possibly can.

Try optimum visualization for at least ten minutes a day. If you have the time, a thirty-minute session is recommended at least three times a week. Keep in mind that this is a form of meditation that requires your absolute commitment of concentrated mind energy. If you just do it whenever you feel like it, or once in a while, the results will be minimal.

The challenge is to try this for twenty-eight days. Start off slow, in ten-minute increments, and build to performing at longer intervals. Your goal is to eventually do this for one hour. Once you are able to sit through a full session and concentrate fully on succeeding in one area of your life, you will have built a solid foundation for personal excellence.

Visualization Action Plan

Simply visualizing isn't enough. You need to take your deepest passions and put them into action by building solid intentions around everything you want to create. In order to do this, you can:

- Use visual meditation for twenty minutes each morning. Visualize the exact reality you want to experience in the future.
- Repeat positive affirmations at the start of each day and again when the day is winding down.
- Create a master goal for your life. Spend twenty to thirty minutes each day imagining the success of this goal. See it in your mind's eye as having already been achieved.
- Play inspirational music to keep you inspired and motivated. As you listen to the music, visualize the activities you are performing that take you closer to fulfilling your vision.
- Practice optimum visualization technique to accomplish amazing results! Plan at least three sessions a week.
- Start a visionary journal or blog and record your thoughts and visions on paper. This enhances your experience of the creative visualization process.
- Create a visual storyboard. You can draw, paint or use pictures to create a collage of your vision.

Build your master vision. Using all of the techniques found in the book or other resource material, continue to build the vision for your life. See yourself as you want to be tomorrow, next year, and in two decades. Apply the power of your visual imagination to making all your dreams come true.

Try the **Forty-Five Minute Power Tri-Combo** by putting together a set of three visualization activities to enhance your imagination. This can include music, meditation, reading, deep thinking, or writing. Try three activities, back to back, for fifteen minutes each.

Write down any negative images that come to mind. Next to those images, write in the positive image that will replace it.

In the next section, you will learn how to build a complete goal portfolio. Our goals play a major role in the direction our lives take and will put you on the path to living the destiny of dreams.

Do you have a plan for the next ten, twenty or thirty years?

If you don't, it's never too late to start building one.

SECTION III:
Goals — Blueprints for Success

"You control your future, your destiny. What you think about comes about. By recording your dreams and goals on paper, you set in motion the process of becoming the person you most want to be. Put your future in good hands—your own."

— Mark Victor Hansen

Pillars of Destiny

"When you discover your mission, you will feel its demand. It will fill you with enthusiasm and a burning desire to get to work on it."

— W. Clement Stone

A goal is a clearly defined statement of what we desire to be and achieve. Goals are the blueprints for success and the building blocks to fulfilling your ultimate dreams. They have the momentum to carry you to places you could only dream about, helping you to achieve substantial results over a long period of time.

A focused goal can transform a simple idea into a multi-million dollar business. It can take a mundane existence and give it purpose, or materialize a dream into reality in just a matter of months. When you create a portfolio of clearly defined goals, this becomes your concrete plan of action for the future.

People with goals are focused, motivated, and opportunistic. People without goals usually end up drifting, wondering what life has in store for them, and they are rarely satisfied.

We have a tremendous storehouse of energy just waiting to be unleashed. The goals you establish for your life become the triggers to unleashing this energy.

Getting Started

Knowing precisely what you want is the first step to making it happen. Once you set your sights on a target, you commit your goals to paper by writing them down and making them real. Then, you will design a plan for success to take you through to the ultimate outcome.

Goal setting has been around for thousands of years, so it's nothing new. But how many people do you know who actually follow through with their goals? How many of your friends, co-workers, or family members have a set of well-defined goals?

How many people do you know who have any kind of plan for their life at all? If you are like me, you know very few. Why? If we know we should be setting goals to create the destiny of our choice, why aren't we doing it?

Set Your Boundaries.

One of the core defining characteristics of people who succeed at winning and achieving goals is the ability to set and stick to boundaries. If we have no boundaries for our goals, we are leaving the door wide open for anyone to walk in and interrupt our focus or steal our time. Your ability to set and stick to specific boundaries is paramount in crushing your goals.

How comfortable are you at telling someone, "No, I can't do that right now. I already have another commitment, and I have to stick to it." If you are like many people, you drop everything when someone you know asks you for something. There urgency becomes your priority.

We have to know where to draw the boundary when it comes to our friends, family, or people in the workplace. When you say "Yes" to something, you are saying "No" to something else. Protecting your time can be critical when you don't have much of it.

Be prepared for resistance when you block the people who don't understand your drive or the motivation behind your actions. They might label you as rude or selfish. If you try to please everyone by doing everything as soon as it lands at your feet, you become a reactive machine, opening the door every time someone has an issue and comes knocking.

Set your boundaries and you will be one of those people that gets your goals finished. What is even better is, you will feel more in control of your life by choosing what to say yes to. People won't like your choices but that is just the way it is. Drawing a line and letting people know where they stand in relevance to your time will give you greater confidence and a feeling of empowerment.

People who set boundaries fail far less than those who don't have any boundaries at all. It's not just the achievement of a goal that matters most—it is the person you become and the positive changes that transform you by reaching this goal.

Achieving the outcome is only part of it. What really matters is who you become when you get there, as well as the skills you develop and the character traits that are strengthened.

The question to ask yourself is this: *Are you planning to fail?*

If there's one lesson that I have learned over the years, it is captured in this statement: If you fail to plan for the future, you plan to fail. You end up contributing to the wealth and happiness of others because you have no plan, and you failed to set any goals.

An Exercise in Goal Writing

Leverage your goals to take control of your life. Before you continue, take out a pen and paper. You are going to perform a valuable exercise that will create momentum for building your goal-management portfolio.

For the next thirty minutes, write down everything you've always wanted to have, do, be, and experience in your lifetime. Don't worry about how crazy it sounds. If it scares you, that's even better. Don't think too hard about how you'll accomplish these things.

In order to create goals that inspire and motivate, they have to be bigger than anything you've tried before. Begin thinking about what it is you'd like to aim for.

On paper, write down where you'd like to go, the skills you want to master, what you want to learn, who you want to meet, and what you desire to build and create. Make a list of all the things you've always dreamed of but could never find the time, energy, or motivation to do. Write for as long as you can and create a list of everything you visualize doing.

Once you are finished, hold on to this list. Tack it up on your wall. Make it visible. This is your springboard for getting started.

A Design For Successful Living

"What you get by achieving your goals is not as important as what you become by achieving your goals."

— Zig Ziglar

You are the architect of your own destiny, and now it's time to begin constructing the pillars of your life. In order to begin, you will need this set of key elements to ensure that your goals have the greatest chance for success.

The 9 Essential Components for Creating Goals

1. A Goal is the Written Word

The first essential ingredient for the success of any goal is to put it into writing. By committing a goal to paper, you are sending a message to the subconscious mind, saying, "Here is what I desire most." Writing your goal down on paper makes it feel more real.

2. A Goal is a Specific, Clear Order

"I want to win the lottery" is not a real goal. "I want to own a new car" is also not a real goal, and neither is, "I want a new job that pays more money." These are only wishes; they are empty desires without any real substance. Before you write anything down, understand that a goal is more than a wish. A goal is a very precise order.

Wishing for something, although fun to do, rarely brings the fortunes you want.

You have to know what you desire. Be clear and specific, as detailed as possible. The more detailed, the better your chances of accomplishing your goal. Instead of simply wanting to buy a house someday, sketch out a picture of the house you want. Make a rough floor plan, or find a picture in a magazine that closely resembles the house you want to live in someday.

Fill in the details with your imagination. The more specific your description, the more likely your dream will materialize.

3. Goals Need a Timeframe

A goal without a deadline is the difference between driving a Porsche to the beach and driving a farm tractor—both will get you there, just within different seasons.

A deadline reminds you there's something that requires your immediate attention. Without a deadline, you are leaving the door open for procrastination—and believe me, it will come in and take over your life if you let it. Before you know it, today becomes tomorrow, and the next thing you know, the goal you wrote down six months ago that should have only taken a few weeks is still waiting for attention.

Once you fix a deadline to your goals, they become more real than you could possibly imagine. No matter how big or far into the future your dream is, always attach a deadline. A workable timeframe is the anchor that holds the goal in place. Without it, your dreams—and enthusiasm—start to float away.

A deadline solidifies your commitment and keeps you motivated and inspired. The deadline is your fixed position. Without it, a goal becomes something you hope you'll get around to eventually.

4. A Goal Has a Plan of Action

Smaller goals contribute to the overall completion of a larger goal. These are sub-goals. Your plan of action will involve many steps that lead to the success of each goal. These steps for success may include research, making phone calls, or sending out applications.

In basic terms, your plan is like a to-do list. It is a list of step-by-step tasks to achieve your goal. By breaking down the steps for each goal, you can manage your time allocated to making progress towards each one.

5. A Goal Requires Channeled Concentration

Spend twenty minutes a day focusing your mind power on a specific task. This form of practice builds up your focused energy. When you get into the deep work of your projects, this will become a very powerful skill.

Spend time each day, at ten-minute intervals, focusing your concentration into the area that is capturing your attention. Focusing on something consciously and with intent applies a force of energy that pushes your thoughts, vision, and ideas toward that goal.

6. A Goal Needs a Solid Commitment

Making a commitment to see a goal through from start to finish can be an extremely daunting task, as well as a test of patience and persistence, especially if the goal is fixed for the long-term. If you are committed to making it happen and you keep that commitment no matter what, you will succeed. You keep pushing forward no matter what obstacles are blocking your path.

When you are committed, nothing can stand in your way for long. You must focus, work with patience, and persist through life's challenges. You must be one hundred percent committed to making it happen.

7. A Goal Needs a Clear Vision

If you are to create the life and results you desire, develop a practice of imagining and visualizing yourself as having already succeeded. How do you feel? What has changed in your life? From sports to the boardroom, every successful achievement is made possible if there is a vision to support it.

Think of your success as having already happened, and the subconscious mind will bridge the gap between the two worlds of the present and what is yet to come. If your goal or mission involves a group of individuals, share your vision with all those involved. A collective group of people working toward a similar goal and sharing a similar vision creates tremendous momentum as each person takes on an essential role.

8. A Goal Needs Accountability

For years I struggled to hit my goals. I failed at deadlines most of the time and didn't enjoy the process of goal setting. But finding an accountability partner changed all of that. An accountability buddy can hold you accountable in so many ways. For example, your accountability partner can:

- Check in on your progress once a week
- Send daily reminders of the master tasks you are working on for the day or week
- Help you celebrate when you hit that goal that has taken you weeks, months or years to achieve

Accountability is a great way to stay on track, stay motivated when you feel like procrastinating, and having someone to talk with about the goals you are working towards. Find an accountability partner to work with and you will not only hit your most important goals but, you'll enjoy the process so much more.

9. The Review

This is probably the most vital step to effectively managing your goal portfolio. By reviewing your goals on a regular basis, you can easily recognize and monitor progress. During the review process, you will...

- Identify pending obstacles blocking your path.
- Review and update your action checklist of tasks required for achieving your goal(s).
- Assess progress and consider whether your deadline is manageable.
- Add any new thoughts or ideas to support continuing progress.

Goal Categories and Building Balance

"All successful people have a goal. No one can get anywhere unless he knows where he wants to go and what he wants to be or do."

— Norman Vincent Peale

Below is a list of categories that represent the level of balance in our lives. Now, with the list of goals you have already created, and using your goal-mapping journal or a notebook, place each category heading at the top of a blank page. Then, list your goals under the proper headings.

Set aside a time frame of ten minutes for each category. Write down everything that comes to mind. Don't be afraid to step out of your comfort zone and get imaginative with your goals.

Family/Child Development/Spousal Relationship

Write down everything that you would like to improve in your life that relates to your relationships. This includes, but is not limited to, your relations with friends, business partners, your spouse, your children, and interactions with the people in your community.

Do you want to...

Marry the partner of your dreams?

- Start a family?

- Send your children to the best university in the country?
- Heal a relationship with a family member?
- Create a closer relationship with your spouse?
- Help your children overcome one of their biggest obstacles?
- Become a family social worker?
- Write a book on child development?
- Take a course in becoming a better parent?

Financial/Investment/Retirement goals

Write down everything that you would like to improve in your life that relates to your financial future.

Would you like to:

- Double your salary over the next year?
- Start the 401K plan you have been putting off?
- Retire early and wealthy?
- Invest in a new business to generate passive income?
- Save enough money for a down payment on your first house?
- Build a solid financial portfolio package?
- Earn $100,000 a year? $1,000,0000? More?
- Start saving 10 percent of your income every month?
- Set up a savings plan for your children?
- Educate yourself on financial planning?
- Pay off your credit card debt?

Health and Exercise/Sports

Write down everything that you would like to improve in your life that relates to your physical condition, mental health, and overall well-being.

Would you like to:

- Win a marathon?

- Compete in a bodybuilding contest?
- Lose weight?
- Power-lift three hundred pounds?
- Join a tennis club and compete in tournaments?
- Become a Major League baseball player?
- Learn martial arts?
- Do a colon cleansing diet?
- Go to a meditation retreat for one week?

How about:

- Becoming an aerobics instructor?
- Opening your own gym or health spa?
- Quitting smoking, drinking, or overcome an addiction?
- Create a new health program to help people change their diet?
- Sell your program to millions of people and health organizations around the world?

Career/Business/Education

Write down goals for building a better career, continued education, and self-development.

Do you want to...

- Open your own retail business or franchise?
- Create a successful online business?
- Start a new career that is in line with your current and future goals?
- Work toward getting a promotion in your field?
- Get interviewed by Business Week?
- Achieve the top sales position in your company?
- Take a course in business administration and change your career path?

For educational goals, would you like to...

- Complete your high school education?
- Get a university degree?
- Learn to speak another language?
- Acquire more advanced skills to land the job of your dreams?
- Become the leader in your industry?

Hobby/Recreational

Write down all the goals for your hobbies and passion projects. Imagine if you had all the time in the world to spend on your hobbies.

Do you want to...

- Learn to paint, draw, or take up another creative hobby?
- Write a novel?
- Build an antique car?
- Learn to swim?
- Learn to build a computer?
- Construct the tree house you always wanted when you were a kid?
- Get your scuba diving license?
- Learn to play a musical instrument?

Travel/World Culture/Adventure

Write down all your goals for traveling, having fun, and living an adventurous lifestyle.

Do you dream of...

- Traveling to Machu Picchu?
- Visiting the Gaza pyramids in Egypt?
- Walking into the Taj Mahal in India?
- Going to Kyoto, Japan and taking a walking tour of the magnificent temples there?
- Traveling to the Sahara Desert?

- Taking a tour of the wildlife parks in Kenya?
- Visiting Stonehenge?
- Traveling to Komodo Island in Indonesia?
- Skydiving in New Zealand?
- Climbing to the Mt. Everest Basecamp?
- Learning to paraglide?
- Sailing around the world?
- Taking a cruise around the ?
- Visiting the resting place of the Titanic
- Walking on the Great Wall of China?
- Learning to fly a helicopter?
- Traveling the world and experiencing new cultures?

Self-Development/Spiritual/ Personal Growth

Write down all the goals for your spiritual growth and personal development.

Would you like to:

- Go on a spiritual retreat?
- Take up yoga and become a yoga master?
- Pursue higher knowledge and practice the art of being through Buddhism?
- Develop a stronger faith in your purpose?
- Strengthen your relationship with a higher power?
- Become a spiritual leader?
- Achieve enlightenment?
- Develop a new character value?

Do you want to...

- Overcome a self-defeating behavior?
- Conquer your greatest fear?
- Change a habit?
- Develop a more positive attitude?

- Become a more positive person and learn to master your mind?

Now that you have your goals written down and you are clear on what you want to achieve in each area of your life, let's move on and identify your power goals within each group.

Creating Your Winning Goals

"Life takes on meaning when you become motivated, set goals and charge after them in an unstoppable manner."

— Les Brown

Now, it's time to create your goals. Retrieve your notes from the brainstorming exercise you did earlier. If you haven't yet done this yet, do it right away. If you have already made a list of your goals, review them and expand on what you have written. You will be mapping out your goals using these essential ingredients.

Put your goals under their proper category listings.

If your goal is to visit the pyramids of Egypt, you might want to put this under the heading World Travel. If your goal is to go to school to become a software engineer, this might go under Career and Business, or Education.

Identify your Power Goal from each category.

Refer to your list of goals. Choose one goal from each category that stands out the most. Which goal from your entire list fills you with such passion and enthusiasm that you can hardly focus on anything else?

Which idea or dream motivates you to take action right now? Once you have identified the super goal from each area, write these goals down on a separate piece of paper.

This will be your **Power Goal** list.

Identify your #1 Power Goal.

Now, from your list of power goals, identify the one goal that means the most to you. It is the one thing, above all else, that you desire to have. Write this power goal in the space provided on the goal creation sheet at the end of this chapter. By identifying this one super goal, you are strengthening the conviction of your great purpose in this life.

What is a Power Goal?

A power goal is your primary target. It is the one goal that will impact your life in substantial ways. This is designed to break you out of your mold and make the unimaginable come true. It is everything you have ever dreamed of doing and becoming.

Your power goal has to be the one thing in life that you have always desired the most. It is your grandest adventure, a seemingly insurmountable obstacle that scares you as much as it excites you. It brings everything in your life into direct alignment with the great purpose that governs all things.

Sub-goals.

Every power goal is divided into smaller actions called sub-goals. Think of it as a piece of cake divided into eight parts; each part represents an important segment of the whole. A goal is the combined effort of many small tasks and actions that, once accomplished, will produce results you want.

Now, write down a list of sub-goals for your number one power goal. If your power goal is to create a superior online business, your sub-goals might include activities like creating a website, developing a product, or building a business team to manage the store.

Smaller steps.

The final step is to break each sub-goal into smaller steps so they are easier to tackle. By breaking them down, you are giving yourself manageable chunks to work with, while reducing stress.

One of the biggest challenges of goal-setting is maintaining a consistent level of organization and self-discipline. Goals are like the plants in your garden: They need regular maintenance. By breaking down the goal into sizeable chunks, it will be easier to track your success.

These smaller steps could include making phone calls, arranging a meeting, or doing research on a particular subject.

Deadline

When you attach a deadline to your power goal, make the deadline reasonable. If your goal is to write a novel and you give yourself until the end of the week to finish it, you are going to disappoint yourself. The deadline should be realistic, flexible, and reasonable.

The deadline is a point of reference for completing a goal. Commit yourself to completing your goal on time, giving it your best shot. Push hard so you can meet your own demands.

You can now attach dates and time limits to your sub-goals, as well, and make a list of tasks to complete these goals. Referring to your list of small steps and tasks, as well as sub-goals, work out how much time you will commit to each step. How long will it take you to write a paper, for example? Do research? Make phone calls? Take a few minutes to write down your estimated timeframe for each goal.

Take Immediate Action

Now that you've committed your goals to paper, added detail and created a workable timeframe, it's time to take action.

In this step, you are igniting your plan. Get started right away!

If you put your goals on paper and then stick them in a drawer someplace, that's probably where they will stay. Take action right away. Do not convince yourself that you have all the time in the world.

Taking action creates positive results and progress. Action breeds more action, and before you know it, you have started some serious momentum toward accomplishing your goals.

Review and Follow-up

The review stage for monitoring your progress is a vital step. Reviewing your goals once a week, once a month, and yearly is the key to keeping them current and ensuring that you move in the direction you want. When you review the status of your active goals, be sure to...

1. Determine the next actions necessary for that week or month.
2. Write down, record, and update any new information, ideas, or insights that contribute to the success of that goal.

By now, your goal portfolio is taking shape. It's a lot of work writing everything down and keeping it organized, but the work you do in the preliminary stage will save you lots of time later. The more planning you do, the easier it will be to achieve your goals.

All my goals have had a deadline. I knew what I wanted from the beginning, and I didn't quit. I knew I would succeed if I stayed committed. It is your level of commitment, persistence, and patience—three very powerful skills to master—that play a key role in the development and creation of the life you want.

If you feel like a mountain climber standing at the bottom of a summit, looking up at the insurmountable obstacle before you, now is the time to use your visualization techniques. You know what you want and you know how to get it. Take the first step and you will be one step closer to victory. Don't turn back. Just keep climbing.

Every step is another victory. Everything carries challenges that seem impossible in the beginning.

Remember, success builds more success. The accomplishment of one goal will lead to the achievement of another. It's like building a house. Before you put the roof on, the rest of the house has to be constructed first.

Think Beyond the Safety Net

One of the biggest errors made when creating goals is having a tendency to go after the easy catch. Instead of setting lofty goals, people set too many limitations. They set easily attainable goals instead of trying for something difficult. They have a tendency to set their standards at a "safe" level to avoid failure or self-disappointment.

Instead of shooting for the stars, they shoot for the nearest cloud and hope they can land safely. If you think only within your own realm of what is possible, your fears will take over and convince you that you've never really accomplished much in the past, so why should you bother now?

Don't listen to the voices that attempt to discourage you. You're capable of anything, as soon as you make the decision and commit. Deep down you know you're capable of anything. Your soul knows this, too, and it wants to shoot high. It doesn't have the same limitations as the mind.

Think of the grandest vision you have for yourself, and focus on that. There will be obstacles to overcome and challenges to face, but you have the support of the universe at your disposal. Tap into that resource and use it efficiently.

Creating Your
Personal Doctrine

*"The more intensely we feel about an idea or
a goal, the more assuredly the idea, buried
deep in our subconscious, will direct us
along the path to its fulfillment."*

— Earl Nightingale

In the previous chapters, you have built the foundation for your future. Now, you'll put everything into a written statement—a personal philosophy for your life's journey.

A personal philosophy statement is a declaration or personal creed. It is a highly focused set of unbroken standards that will be the foundation for the beliefs, values, and principles that govern the discipline of your daily life.

This philosophy of life is a focused statement that carries you toward the achievement of your goals. It acts as your guiding compass.

This is a contract with yourself, a written doctrine that serves as the code of ethics for your personal character development. This also establishes a set of concrete values.

The framework of your personal philosophy statement serves to uphold your deepest values. It governs everything you aspire to achieve under a set of clearly defined goals.

Your great purpose for living is put into action in everything you do, and your personal philosophy establishes the laws by which you will live.

Your thoughts are channeled through a system of integrated thinking, and the vision you build through the product of imagination stays within this focused arena. It becomes the deepest expression of who you are and clarifies the meaning of your life. When executed with commitment and responsibility, it carves a direct path to mastery and excellence, and works to support all fields of life.

The philosophy of life, or personal mission statement, is the foundational center from which everything flows. Your vision for who you want to be, the differences you want to make, the contributions and services you want to deliver—everything flows from the core of this personal philosophy.

Consider writing your philosophy utilizing these key areas:

Contribution

This is the area in which you can make a difference to people and organizations in your life. It defines how will you contribute and be of service toward:

- Your family
- Your friends and personal relationships
- Your employers and professional communities
- The global community

Write out a statement for each heading and clearly define how you are going to contribute to each of the areas listed above.

Core Values

By developing a self-awareness of the values you cherish, you will identify who you are and what you believe. Your values express personal uniqueness and help you make future decisions.

Your vision is supported by your values. To get started, review the list below. Create a list of your own core values, and prioritize them in order of importance. Once you have your priority list, choose the one value that has the greatest importance to you.

Honesty, integrity, forgiveness, surrender, understanding, sacrifice, excellence, trustworthiness, empathy, humility, tolerance, loyalty, nobility, trustworthiness, spirituality, wisdom, self-discipline, peace, equality, traditionalism, adventure, success, financial independence, wealth, security, gratitude/thankfulness, respect, reliability, awareness, consciousness, persistence, success, health, passion, mastery, leadership, kindness, imagination, happiness, uniqueness, popularity, winning, adaptability, change, friendship, love, empowerment, character growth, patience, self-expression.

Goals

Take some time to look over the goals you have set for yourself. Write down your first primary goal. Then, choose two more goals.

Primary Goal 1:

Primary Goal 2:

Primary Goal 3:

Are these goals in alignment with your vision and values?

Vision

Clearly define the vision you have for the life you desire to create. Find a quiet place, and take twenty minutes to imagine your life and the person you'll evolve into over the years. Add detail to this vision and see everything within your mind's eye. Tap into your deepest imagination and maintain that vision for as long as you can.

Now, write down what you visualize as your future reality. Write it down in the present tense as if it's already happening.

Empowering Beliefs

What are the beliefs that contribute to your purpose and are in alignment with the values and principles you have established? Here are a few examples of beliefs I have selected:

- I believe in the strength and goodness of humanity.
- I believe in forgiving others for their mistakes and imperfections.
- I believe the universe is a sacred place that provides answers to any questions we have.
- I believe I can do anything, and that the only limitations that exist are in my mind.
- I believe I am here for a reason, and that those reasons are unfolding in the thoughts and actions I engage in every day.

Life Roles

Each of us has several roles that make up our commitments and responsibilities to family, work, and relationships in general. These are the roles that define our level of service to the environment we have created. Some people have one or two main roles, while others have eight or more. Regardless of how many roles you are responsible for fulfilling, each has a level of importance.

Here is a sample list of roles you may be familiar with:

Husband, father, wife, mother, friend, community spokesperson, company president, employee, teacher, coach, writer, musician, student, doctor, volunteer

Take a moment to write down the roles you are responsible for and include your function in each role, what the role means to you, and how you contribute to each role.

Action List

What actions can you take to ensure that your life stays on track?

The actions I will take are:

- Creating a daily/weekly/monthly action list
- Reading affirmations that empower my spirit
- Keeping my workspace organized and clean
- Avoiding distractions and activities that lead to lethargy
- Concentrating and staying focused on my goals twice a day

Accomplishments/Victories

What are the results you hope to achieve? By following the course of my personal philosophy statement, and staying focused on the values, principles, goals, and vision for my life, I hope to:

- Make a difference in the lives of those around me.
- Become more professional in my career.
- Develop a higher level of spiritual awareness and consciousness.
- Become financially independent.
- Strengthen my role as a parent through understanding my children's emotional needs and wants.
- Develop a deeper relationship with my wife, my children, and my friends.
- Accomplish my greatest dream.

Now, make a list of the accomplishments you are going to achieve through living your life according to your personal philosophy statement.

Your Personal Philosophy Statement

Using the information you've already outlined, you are going to create your personal philosophy statement. Before you do, take some time to think about these questions and write about them in your notebook.

1. How would you define the person you want to evolve into by the end of your life?
2. What brings you the greatest sense of joy and fulfillment?
3. What are three things you've always wanted to do with your life?
4. How are you going to make a difference in the city/town/community you live in?
5. What is the vision you have of the life you will be living twenty years from today?
6. What habits do you need to change to put you in alignment with your personal philosophy statement?

7. What are the master roles in your life, and how will you work to empower these roles in the future?
8. How would you define the meaning and purpose of your life?
9. What is your primary life goal?

Now, utilizing everything you have brainstormed in the previous exercises, write out your personal philosophy statement. Rewrite it several times, until it clearly defines everything that encompasses your life as a whole. In the weeks and months to come, feel free to revise your statement when necessary.

Stick To Your Guns

"When we are motivated by goals that have deep meaning, by dreams that need completion, by pure love that needs expressing–then we truly live life."

— **Greg Anderson**

Your goals are now in writing and explained in concrete detail, with a deadline, and backed up by a solid plan of immediate action to start the momentum. You know what you want and you are filled with a burning passion to charge forward. You are even waking up early to get a head start on the day and you feel like nothing can stop you. You know exactly what you want and you're going to get it.

Then, after a short while, something changes. The excitement you felt a couple months ago has diminished and you feel yourself being pulled in other directions. The goal you were once so focused on has become nothing but a distant blur. You have stopped reviewing your goals and have fallen back into a pattern of sloth and helplessness. Everything seems lost.

Staying On Track

It appears that the world and everyone in it has their own agenda. You feel derailed and cheated. This is part of the ongoing challenges you will face. You must learn to deal with it as it happens. Family matters must be attended to, your boss wants a report on his desk by yesterday, and it seems as if no matter how hard you try to stay focused on the big picture, other forces with hidden agendas are pulling you off course.

Well, this is the reality of life and it doesn't just step aside while we pursue other interests, galloping into the sunset, seeking our glory and fortune. You have to mold yourself into the reality of the world around you because the world is unforgiving when it comes to our own personal needs. If you find yourself losing interest or drifting away from the excitement of the goals you have set, the important thing is to stick with it, especially when the going gets tough.

There will be days and weeks when you have had so many setbacks that you'll want to throw in the towel and walk away. Those who give up often fail to realize they were already within sight of the finish line, but too blinded by other distractions to notice.

There are so many things that demand our attention and test our patience and strength of conviction. This is reality, and losing your focus is all part of the process.

There are ways to get through the tough times. The trick with goal management is to envision your victory first. Think about it every day. Imagine it. Feel it. Meditate on it and think with deep focus about what it is you're trying to achieve. Someday, when you look back on the hard times, you can say, "I am here today because I didn't give up." Others will look back and say, "If only I hadn't given up." Choose which side you want to be on.

No matter what frustrations you face, remind yourself that this is your plan, your life, and your future. You are making it happen with the victory of living each day to its fullest. Days of futility will be remembered as tough but educational. It is through the hard times that our success is born.

Staying on the right course means more than just managing your goals; it's about managing yourself as well. If you can manage your affairs, stay persistent, keep your priorities straight, you will excel at everything you focus on.

Remember, success is the result of facing the obstacles that block your path. Those who never give up and stay on course in the face of adversity will experience more than they have ever dreamed. Here is a list of suggestions for sticking with it.

1. Stay persistent in the face of failure

The greatest battles in history have been won because the victors refused to give up. Failure was not an option. If you fall down once, get up. If you fall down, get up. If you stay down, you'll fail, and what could have been your success will become someone else's victory.

The key to success is persistence, and every successful entrepreneur will tell you that success is the combined effort of dozens of failures. When you want to succeed so badly that nothing else matters, quitting is not an option. You will find a way to make it work. You pay the price for the required sacrifice and push on. Don't give up when the finish line is right in front of you.

2. Stay consistent with learning

The consistency of practicing a skill or habit leads to the mastery of new abilities. Work consistency into your daily life. Make it a priority and practice what you want to perfect. Remember, the key to mastering anything is to perform the action again and again, not just when you feel like it, but in a consistent pattern that builds the habit. This leads to the mastery of a skill. Consistency plus persistence equals success.

3. Make the right friendships

If you want to stop gambling, don't hang around the casinos looking for new friends. If you want to quit smoking or drinking, stay away from bars and all related activities that promote these habits. In other words, surround yourself with the support that is necessary for your success, as well as the success of others. Keep your support group close, and if you don't have a support group, find one.

Having people in your life to share thoughts and ideas with is a powerful method for staying on track. People, who understand what you're trying to do and want to contribute to your mission, or join you to succeed on your journey, will become powerful allies.

Success is rarely accomplished alone. Friends, business partners, or family members can add a lot of weight to your success. As you succeed and raise the quality of your own life, you raise the bar for everyone. Who wouldn't want to be a part of that?

4. Take one action every day

As soon as your goals are set, get busy! People with ambition are never bored. We always have something to work on, even if it's a small task. The achievement of a goal is a daily effort.

On the days you don't feel like doing anything, even ten minutes working at something can account for a lot. If you take two or three days off, this leads into a week, and then a month, and before you know it you've lost sight of everything. It's happened to me several times, and it was a lot of work to pull myself back on track because I had derailed so far.

Do something every day that contributes to your future. Don't worry about doing it perfectly. Your actions will stimulate the motivation you need.

5. Read material that influences you

Motivation is like a wave; it rises and falls. When you have a bad day during which you don't accomplish much, find something stimulating to read.

Listed below are my recommendations for personal development. Some of these books have helped me, and when I felt lost, the wisdom and advice of others paved a brighter path for me. Read the works of people who encourage you, because it will have a profound impact on the way you think and feel.

Here are some reading recommendations:

1. The One Thing by Gary Keller

2. Do It Scared by Scott Allan

3. Awaken the Giant Within by Tony Robbins

4. A New Earth: Awakening to Your Life's Purpose by Eckhart Tolle

5. Essentialism: The Disciplined Pursuit of Less by Greg McKeown

6. The Miracle Morning: The 6 Habits That Will Transform Your Life (Before 8 AM) by Hal Elrod

7. Living Forward: A Proven Plan to Stop Drifting and Get the Life You Want by Michael Hyatt and Daniel Harkavy

8. The Art of Work: A Proven Path to Discovering What You Were Meant to Do by Jeff Goins

9. The 7 Habits of Highly Effective People: Powerful Lessons in Personal Change by Stephen R. Covey

10. The Power of Positive Thinking: 10 Traits for Maximum Results by Dr. Norman Vincent Peale

11. The Success Principles by Jack Canfield

12. Habit Stacking by S.J. Scott

6. Keep track of your progress

A lofty goal could take as long as five, ten, or even twenty years to reach. Most people find it a challenge to maintain that much patience or level of persistence. This is why we need to monitor our success as it is happening. The completion of a goal, after all, is a combination of all the little things you are doing every day.

You can start by making a list of all the short tasks and small goals you are going to accomplish for the week. Make a plan and try to stick with it by performing small tasks daily. Print out your list of tasks and tack it on your wall.

At the end of the week, when you are finished with that piece of paper, file it away. Don't get rid of it. You want to be able to look back at your task sheet and see that you have been making progress as the action steps you achieved are crossed off. Keeping score will make you feel good. You can see the progress happening because it's measurable.

My suggestion is to put aside ten minutes a night to read your goals over and make a plan of action for the following day. Then, monitor your progress and keep score of your achievements.

7. Keep a goal-mapping journal

A goal-mapping journal is a great way to keep track. Several years ago, I started a goal-mapping journal, and to this day I use it to measure where I am, as well as update and add new entries whenever I need to.

A goal-mapping journal is used to record your intentions. You'll use this to list your dreams and goals. I like to use goal-setting templates. Then, using tape or glue, I will fix the template inside my goal-mapping journal.

For some goals I include magazine or Internet pictures, as well as any articles or sources of interest about the goal I have. A goal-mapping journal keeps things neat and tidy. It's also a great way of staying on track.

Goal Building Action Plan

1. Looking back over your goals, how do you feel about what you have written down? Do you feel energized and excited about the path you detailed for yourself? Is there anything you want to change right now? If so, take the time to think about it and alter your goals.

2. What is your lifetime goal? What is the deadline you have set for this goal? What category does this goal fall under? Write down as much detail as you can.

3. What is your number one power goal for this year? What is your number two power goal? What is your plan for reaching these goals? Describe them here.

4. Have you shared your goals with anyone else? If so, what was their reaction?

Is there someone you know who could use your help? Is this person interested in what you are working on? If so, what can you do to help them?

5. What are the special skills you need to develop before you can achieve one or more of your goals? Is more research necessary?

6. What are some goals that you've already accomplished? Were they important to the purpose in life that you have now?

7. Sit quietly for ten minutes and give yourself time and space to think about this. Imagine yourself twenty years from now. You are looking back at what you have accomplished.

Imagine that you have succeeded at many of your goals and your life has changed incredibly—and so have you.

How does this make you feel? Spend ten minutes every evening visualizing this.

Destiny Builders Checklist

- Commit your goal to paper. Write a brief statement about the goal.
- Create a working list of steps necessary for achieving this goal.
- Visualize the goal coming true.
- Create a deadline.
- Place the goal into a category.
- Define the desired result(s) of achieving your goals.
- Monitor and track your progress.
- Review your progress.
- Revise your goals on a regular basis.
- Describe the expected life impact of achieving your goals.
- Describe who you will become after achieving a lifelong goal of significant importance.
- Create a personal philosophy statement.

SECTION IV:
Building Better Habits

"Your net worth to the world is usually determined by what remains after your bad habits are subtracted from your good ones."

— Benjamin Franklin

Habits of Destiny

"Chains of habit are too light to be felt until they are too heavy to be broken."

— Warren Buffet

Your habits, for better or for worse, have had a massive impact on defining who you are today. The habits you focus on will determine who you become in the future and the kind of work you do. Habits, and the repetitive actions that make them, will ultimately define the quality of your lifestyle, for today and in your future.

Habits don't just happen. They are formed from a young age, and will transition throughout your lifetime. But if you just let your habits "happen to you" rather than choosing the habits you need, you will become a slave to your circumstances. You cannot be in charge of your destiny if you are not in control of the habit that governs your actions.

We have to create a pattern of consistent actions that move us closer to our dreams and goals.

How can we do this?

First, by making yourself aware of the good and bad habits you have. You might have more good than bad, or vice versa. Either way, by replacing (not eliminating) your bad habits, you can open up the channels for better productivity, less stress, and alleviate the frequency of your boredom cycles.

For example, I have a strong desire to wake up early every morning. Why? I want to write a book, and I can use that time to write. But if I am used to waking up at 6:30 every morning, getting up at five a.m. will be challenging. I might struggle and find an excuse for not getting up early. Chances are, if I try to do this, I'll end up hitting the snooze button and sleeping until I am ready to get up, which is usually 6:30. But I could get up at six.

So, I start small. I don't start by waking up at five on the first day. I start by waking up fifteen minutes earlier. You can even try ten minutes earlier each day.

What are the kind of habits we should be focusing on?

If you hold the desire to be a wealthy person, you must forge the behavioral habits that create wealth. If your desire is to create change in the world, your habits must be in alignment with the right actions to create these changes.

Positive habits, such as exercising and eating well, create richer lives. Poor habits, such as smoking or impulsive shopping, can lead you to poverty in both health and personal finances.

The Repetition of Habit

Through consistency, you can have life-shaping experiences. Your habits are the thick roots of destiny. When molded in childhood, habits transform our lives in countless ways, affecting life-making decisions and future events. Good habits form character, broaden your mindset, and generate positive energy to reduce stress and anxiety.

The nature of any habit is repetition. The force of that habit is decided by the results you get from the action. If you have a bad habit or an addiction such as gambling, your reward is the euphoric high you feel when you win. But the result is that you could lose all your money.

A better habit would be to invest your money. While you may not see the return on your investment as quickly as you would from winning a game, over time you'll be rewarded. The nature of your success depends on the habits you feed.

First of all, a behavior is only a bad habit if it harms you in some way. While most bad habits are obvious, such as smoking or gambling excessively, we continue to do them because of the perceived reward.

You might spend money frivolously, leaving nothing at the end of the month because of the high you get from buying something. Compare that to someone else who has saved their money, putting away just five dollars per day. At the end of the year, they can fulfill one of their dreams, such as taking a trip to Europe.

The habits you adopt have a direct influence on the fulfillment you experience in your life. Habits provide a sense of order and organized structure to daily living, regardless of whether they're good or bad.

Similar to our DNA, your habits are a unique part of you. While we can't change our DNA, we can change our habits.

Habits designed specifically with your purpose and core objectives serve to help you in ways that nothing else can. How you think, how you act and react, how you work, and how you respond to your emotions serves as the benchmark for what you'll achieve, who you will become, and where you're going to end up.

In order for us to master anything in this world, it is imperative that we first learn to master our habits. Whether you consider yourself a success, a failure, or a mediocre achiever, your habits have played a powerful role in the path you have chosen for yourself.

If you can accept this, you can realize this one important point: You're either in control of your habits, or your habits are in control of you. Unfortunately, many people fail to master their lives because they never gain control of their habits.

If your goal is to make lasting changes in your life, you have to gain control of your most prominent habits. You have to remove the repetitive and damaging actions holding you back and replace them with massive, mind-blowing habits that generate real results.

Habits can be molded, and how you mold them is up to you. Your habits build character, and then your character builds your life.

In the first section of this book, we looked at the vision you have for your life and how critical this is. As important as it is, your vision needs action, and those actions can be found in your daily habits.

Just as they can provide us with everything we've ever wanted, a lack of positive habits leads to lethargy, poor decisions, confusion, wasted time, and self-destructive behavior. Feeding into this chaos leaves you with weak choices and limitations that lead to undesirable results.

Think about the people in your life. What habits are they implementing? Are they in control of their habits, or are the habits controlling them? What habits do you have that you're controlling? What do you struggle with?

Answering these questions can help you focus on the habits that matter, training your mind to cut away at those habits that derail your focus and productivity.

Building Positive Habits

A habit is a learned action acquired through conditioned responses that take years to build. You can choose to act out the habits you have always had and achieve the same repetitive results. Or you can try new things by taking the initiative to build a set of actions that lay the foundation for new patterns. In doing so, you choose to live the life you want instead of being conditioned to live the one you don't need.

Many people have the desire to change and do something different, but they fail to change the habits that lead them to certain failure. The level of success you will achieve in your lifetime is easy to predict; just look at your present habits and you will know exactly what you'll end up with.

Excessive TV watching, excessive shopping, and excessive pleasure-seeking devices become the standard for out of control patterns that lead to dead ends. Either gain control of your daily habits, or you will be controlled by them, and they will damage your self-esteem and confidence.

We form habits that waste time and trap us in a system of repetition that we later regret.

Some of these habits could include:

- Watching TV in excess

- Smoking

- Trolling the Internet with your smartphone

- Eating junk food

- Playing video games for over three hours a week

- Impulsive shopping

- Complaining about your family, friends, and coworkers

There are two types of habits—**passive** and **active**. We don't have to think about passive habits. They are so ingrained in us that a decision isn't required to take action. For example, if brushing your teeth after dinner is something you have been doing for twenty years, this is a passive habit. As long as a passive habit isn't causing you any harm, there's no need to change it. Besides, brushing your teeth is always a good thing.

Another passive habit could be watching television every night. It is so ingrained in you that you turn the TV on as soon as you get home from work. The next day you get up and go to work again. Again, there's nothing wrong with this routine—unless you are miserable and you want to change it. If so, you know that you have the ability and the choice to turn any habit around.

Forging Habits for Lasting Success

"Change might not be fast and it isn't always easy. But with time and effort, almost any habit can be reshaped."

— **Charles Duhigg**, author of
The Power of Habit

The moment you stop letting life happen to you and start making things happen, you have the advantage. Instead of saying, "I'll just wait and see what happens next," take a position of power in your life, make a proactive choice, and say, "This is what's going to happen!" Make a habit out of taking charge.

Ask yourself whether you want to live the remainder of your existence doing the things you've always done, using the same worn-out habits that bring the same disappointing results. Or would it make more sense to adopt a new way of thinking, a different way to respond to circumstances and people instead of letting the situation dictate your next step?

In this section, we're going to cover the habit-building process, and then learn how we can eliminate habits that keep us from living our destiny.

You don't have to live in the past anymore. Whatever you did or didn't do, however you may have lived your life yesterday, the only thing that matters now is how you live today. Are you ready to commit to creating a powerful mental highway that provides new experiences, choices, and emotions?

The Power of Repetition: Building Blocks of Destiny

Through building a system of actionable habits, you will be able to think more clearly and stay focused on your objectives without getting distracted.

By building a new habit that is in direct line with your goals and values, you can gain control of your life. Through constructing a system of new habits and actionable patterns, you can replace outdated thought patterns and train your mind to act in accordance with your values.

You can identify what matters and ignore what is irrelevant. Many people fail because they have built a pattern of habits that bring trouble. These are habits that are reactionary, and they will fail you. A reactive habit means you're reacting without intention.

By building powerful, repetitive habits, you are laying down the foundation for a new life. Habits practiced with consistency create opportunities that never would have existed otherwise.

You can change anything in your life if you stick to these steps:

- Know what you want to achieve.

- Know the reasons why you're on this path.

- Know how you'll accomplish what you're trying to do.

- Continue to reinforce new patterns on a consistent basis.

- Continue to substitute old behaviors for healthier choices.

- Review your current actions and habits on a regular basis.

Follow these steps and you will acquire the skills to transform your life. But first you must acquire the habit, and the habit, once formed into an unbreakable chain, will bring what you desire.

Constructing a System of Good Habits

Let's take a few minutes to do a simple exercise. I want you to make a list of habits you're willing to change today. I use the word willing because—even if you fail at your first attempts—as long as you keep trying, your chances of success increase with every failure.

Negative habits are rarely changed in the first few attempts. We have to keep trying. With every effort, you are strengthening the cords of repetition. Eventually, the cords become unbreakable cables.

In a notebook, create a page with two sides. On the left side, make a list of habits you desire to give up. On the right side, adjacent to each habit, write down the method you are going to apply to reinforce the change. You only have to write down one method for now. There could be a lot of actions to take, but we only need one. You can work on expanding this later.

For instance, if you're willing to stop smoking, just stopping cold turkey isn't enough. It might work for some people, but for many it's a tough way to quit. You have to replace the habit with something else, such as following through on a new workout routine.

If you want to get into the habit of saving money instead of spending it, just wanting to save may not work. Most people would like to save more. Few people actually follow through. Why? They aren't willing to make the necessary changes to their daily spending habits.

If your habit is impulse buying, there are two actions you must consider. First you have to break the pattern of compulsive shopping, and then you need to replace it with a new action that involves saving your cash instead of spending it.

As you do this exercise, follow the steps I recommend for making changes. Through sticking with these steps, I have broken countless habits that would have ruined me physically, financially, and mentally. Be the master of your world from this day forth, but first, gain control of actions that influence these habits.

Good habits build new worlds and give rise to a new way of living, whereas existing in a state of compulsive action and out-of-control, chaotic behavior leads you away from your destiny.

Your world, the life you constructed, has largely been influenced by the habits you have adhered to all these years. For good or bad, habits have built your life.

Replacing old, worn-out habits and limiting patterns is the key to obtaining long-term success. However, just stopping something isn't enough. Without replacing the old habit with a new pattern, your chances of success are minimal.

Old patterns, even after years of absence, still have active roots in the soils of your mind. The only thing it takes to invite those old ways back is a thought or action leading to reinforcement of the dead pattern. Before you know it, you're right back where you started.

Addiction is a perfect example. Those who relapse, even after years of abstinence, venture back to what's most familiar even though it almost destroyed them. Even after years of staying on course, if we are not diligent in sticking with our newly formed habits, the bad habits that caused us grief will return, and in greater force this time.

The habits you've changed, although no longer so powerful, still have invisible threads attached to your psyche. Like the roots of a dead tree, they linger beneath the surface, waiting to be called back into action.

Be aware of their presence, and after years of positive reinforcement and changes, if you feel yourself being pulled back into old patterns, identify the root of the issue right away. Is it a thought, a feeling, or an action you performed? Did you meet someone who triggered feelings from the past? Was it a certain song you heard?

There could be any number of reasons. Take the time to review where you are. Once you identify the cause, you become stronger because you'll be able to close the door and sever the connection with the old pattern before it becomes active again.

Elements for Creating Positive Habits

Purpose - Why do you want to change? What do you hope to accomplish through this change? What positive influence will converting this habit bring to you? How will this change benefit others? If you don't have a purpose for change that motivates and drives you forward, your chances of converting a habit are slim.

Define the reasons why you absolutely must change a pattern of behavior, give yourself powerful reasons why, and you will increase your success factor. A weak purpose only inspires a weak effort, whereas a purpose that motivates and excites you creates powerful momentum that inspires desire.

Desire - When it comes to creating new pathways for habits, a powerful desire to change is critical. The only time I have been successful at changing anything, it was because I truly wanted to change it.

You can have a reason to change, and know how to go about it, but it must be something you want and not what someone else wants. Have you ever tried to change for someone else, and even though you might have succeeded, you still felt miserable?

This is because you have to want it more than anything else. Desire is fueled by purpose. See the changes you are making in your life and visualize the powerful results these changes are bringing. Visualize the world you are creating through developing and initiating habits that align with your truest values.

Letting go - What would you be willing to give up in exchange for everything you've always wanted? What cravings, temptations, or addictions would you have to surrender in order to have everything you truly desired? What is your happiness and the happiness of your loved ones worth? What sacrifices will you make to succeed?

Methods - To change your habits, there are certain methods you can use. Ask yourself what habits you'll need to develop to accomplish your goals. What are the steps you'll take from now on to convert these internal pathways to serve your purpose?

Write down the constructive habits you want to have and the steps you'll take to develop them. In order to succeed, you have to know what methods you'll use. There must be a plan for success. Remember, failing to know how you will succeed (creating a plan) is planning to fail.

Identifying the new habits you want is the critical step to making real changes in your life. Right now, write down a habit that you want to convert. Then write down the habit that will take its place.

Using the habit conversion sheet, take the challenge to change this habit through a steady, consistent focus of your energy. Don't think about failing. You can't fail this. Make small changes through daily practice. Turn to the habit conversion challenge sheet and get started on making real, positive changes in your life.

Now, here are the fourteen action steps you can take to make sure you are creating a system of habits that are working for you. Consider this a checklist, but you don't have to carry out every step perfectly.

Your Habit Destiny Program

"I never could have done what I have done without the habits of punctuality, order, and diligence, without the determination to concentrate myself on one subject at a time."

— Charles Dickens

When it comes to habit building, we can break it down into two stages:

1. Build your new habit slowly.
2. Break the bad habit gradually.

For example, I was in the habit of consuming large amounts of sugar every day. This consisted of a chocolate bar, ice cream, and various sweets. When I decided to stop this bad habit and replace it with better foods, I cut my chocolate intake by half the first week. Then, I cut it again in half for the second week. By the third week of cutting down gradually, I was hardly craving it.

When it came to watching TV, I knew I had to reduce television time in order to do more writing, reading, and meditating. So I approached watching TV the same way I eliminated chocolate. I scheduled my movie time at certain periods of the week so that it eliminated the impulse to turn on the TV whenever I felt like it.

1. Visualize living the new habit

A new habit can be hard to instill in yourself, but imagine how it will change your life. How would you look and feel after three months of steady exercise? Where would your career be if you dedicated thirty minutes a day to reading books on building a business? How would you change mentally and emotionally if you were meditating for ten minutes every day?

In the first part of this book, we discussed visual imagination. You can use this tactic for forming new habits. Say you want to lose weight, but you have a habit of eating junk food every night. You can visualize what you'll look like after dropping twenty pounds. You can visualize the habit of exercising in the evening instead of just watching TV and consuming junk. In doing so, you will create the emotions that go with it.

2. Focus on the daily action, and not the end goal

It is easy to focus on the end goal. But it doesn't stop there. If you form the habit of eating less junk food and more greens so that you can lose thirty pounds, what happens when you reach your goal? You mind could trick you into thinking, "This is it," and revert back to your old routine again.

Keep setting new goals for yourself so that you're always improving. Stay fixed on what you can achieve each day. Be realistic, as well. Instead of deciding you'll lose twenty pounds, stay focused on not eating junk food for today, or doing twenty minutes of cardio exercise.

3. Focus on one habit at a time

There are dozens of habits we could try to change next week. Habits we want to break, and habits we want to start. I would recommend focusing on one new habit until it is fixed. Then you can scale up and start another one.

Can you imagine where you would be in six months if you committed to just one course of action? Focusing on one habit can have a tremendous impact. If you try to change several habits at once, you'll become frustrated when you start to miss a day here and there, and then one failure becomes many. One habit is a manageable goal.

4. Create an action plan for each habit and repeat

The goal is to commit to a set action plan for each day. This can be as simple as committing to five minutes per day doing a single action. For example, If you're trying to build the exercise habit, you can do just five reps on the first day. If you are writing a book, commit to writing for ten minutes for the next thirty days.

What matters isn't how much we get done. The idea is to follow through with the action and make it a consistent pattern you perform everyday, regardless if it is ten reps or fifty. You can scale up later when you are conditioned to doing the action without thinking about it.

5. Repeat this action every day for the next thirty days

You can commit to the same time each day, which is the best situation. For example, write two hundred words of your novel first thing in the morning at six a.m. Meditate for ten minutes every evening an hour before bed.

If you think about it, you already perform hundreds of habits a day unconsciously at roughly the same time each day. Now, we're making ourselves aware of the new habit by pushing it into our schedule and making it a regular occurrence.

6. Be realistic in your expectations

Change takes time. We have to be patient with our progress and resilient in our approach. The people who become masters at what they do reach that level through decades of practice. Tony Robbins said, "We overestimate what we can do in a month but underestimate our progress in a year."

If you have had the same habit for years, it is deeply ingrained into your mind. Expecting to replace your habit with a new one takes time, and it could take up to six months. Even then, you have to continue practicing the new habit.

7. Keep it simple

Habit building isn't complicated. You can keep it simple by trying the following:

- Focus on one habit a time.
- Perform the same action every day.
- And at the same time every day.
- Scale up gradually.
- Measure your results.

8. Create your habit triggers

Set up a trigger for your new habit. This works for both creating new ones and breaking your bad habits. For example, if your new habit is to read for ten minutes a day, leave the book you are reading on the table in the morning so that it's the first thing you see.

Whatever your focus is for building this habit, you can leave it out in the morning, or set an alarm to go off at a certain time each day. For example, I scheduled my habit time in my calendar. That way I would receive a notification when it was time to take action.

The trigger becomes your permission to take action. Make it visible. Make it so loud that you can't ignore it.

9. Be aware of bad habit triggers

Just as we need triggers to take action toward positive habits, we also need to be aware of the triggers that pull us back into bad habits. For example, when I reduced the amount of junk food I was eating, I had a habit of trolling through the junk food aisle in the store. As soon as I walked into the store it was the first section I visited. Then, if they were having a sale on chocolate that day, my trigger would associate cheap chocolate with pleasure, and I would give in.

Whatever habit you're working on replacing, make yourself aware of the habits that trigger you to give in and eat, spend, or indulge. The danger lies in our own minds. It is your thinking that causes you to seek out the trigger spot. You might be working on replacing smoking with exercise, and then after a workout, you stroll by a cigar shop because it's on your way home.

In the early stages of habit changing, we are vulnerable to our cravings and what a mentor of mine called "crooked thinking." Make yourself aware of the habits that draw you into relapsing.

People relapse all the time, in many cases because the old habit returns when they don't get results after a week or two. We then unconsciously seek out our old routines because they are familiar. New habits have a certain level of discomfort until they become solidified.

If you relapse, try again. The key is to focus on daily positive action.

10. Set daily, easy to hit target goals

Let's say our decision is to create a habit for reading more books. This would increase your knowledge and would be a better activity than watching TV. If you stick with thirty minutes of reading per day, you could read five books in a month. But if thirty minutes is a tough habit to stick with, try just ten minutes a day. This is easily manageable.

In fact, most habits could be built in just five to ten minutes per day. You don't have to invest an hour every day or push yourself to the end of exhaustion.

Break it down into small chunks and you'll have created your new habit within thirty days. You want to write a book? Start with one hundred words per day. You want to wake up earlier? Start by setting your alarm ten minutes earlier. You could also build a habit to go to bed earlier. Remember it's not the big result that we're going for, but building the behavior. Once you master the routine, you can scale up at any time.

11. Focus on long-term conversion

It takes time to change behaviors. If it happened quickly, everyone would be doing it. According to a study released in the *European Study of Social Psychology* a team of researchers led by **Phillippa Lally** surveyed ninety-six people over twelve weeks to find out how long it took them to develop a new habit. At the end of the survey, Lally analyzed the results of the experiment and determined the time it took to form a new habit was approximately sixty-six days.

We need to think long-term. It takes approximately sixty-six days to replace a habit. This is a tough road to navigate for most people.

We need long-term focus and consistent concentration over a period of months to make it happen. If you are expecting to see massive gains after two weeks, you could be setting yourself up to fail. Think long-term habit change, and stay focused on daily repetitions.

An example would be pushups. I do fifty to seventy-five pushups four times per week. But it took me nearly three months to build up to this. I started by doing five a day for the first week, then ten a day in the second week. Then, I increased by two push-ups a day until I hit my goal of fifty a day. Every day I would add two more to the habit. By focusing on the long-term objective, which was to build up to one hundred a day, I could achieve this and get into better shape than ever before.

Action Plan:

Have a long-term focus and scale up slowly. Whatever your habit, you can achieve your goal by scaling slowly. Stay fixed on the behavior.

12. Focus on habit replacement instead of elimination

When it comes to building new habits, our initial thought is, "I have to eliminate the old habits." If you want to eat healthier to lose weight and get into better shape, eliminating junk food intake isn't a realistic plan. Instead, focus on reducing the habit a little bit every week.

Reduce your sugar intake every day by ten percent. You'll have less pressure to do it perfectly. You can apply this to any habit you are attempting to break. Want to reduce the amount of time you spend online? Start cutting down by five percent a day. You can set up blocks of time when you're offline altogether instead of wired to your cellphone or computer.

To get away from constantly looking at your cell phone, consider buying a regular alarm clock and a watch. This will prevent you from using your phone as an alarm, and keep you from looking at it as soon as you wake up. Now that you have a watch, you won't need to check your phone for the time—which means you won't get distracted by other notifications on your screen, either.

Action Plan:

Reduce your habits by five percent a day. Don't simply eliminate. Then you can hit your goals much more realistically. Focus on reduction, not elimination.

13. Build support through accountability

New habits are difficult to implement and stick with, especially in the beginning. For this reason, having a habit buddy is a recommended approach to supporting your new routine.

If you're trying to get into the habit of exercising more, this could be someone you go jogging with twice a week, or you might do strength training together. If you can't meet in person, you can connect via Zoom, Skype, or Google Hangouts.

Set up a habit accountability call with your friend once a week to follow up on progress. Make sure you work with someone who is also interested in habit development, although they could be working on a different habit. It's important to share not just the fun of habit building, but the struggles you are going through as well.

Action Plan:

Find a habit support buddy. Connect once per week—online, on the phone, or in person—to discuss your progress or any difficulties you've experienced.

14. Throw out the all or nothing approach

If you've had a slip, get back into it. We all miss a day in our routine. What matters is that you can pick it up again the next day. If you let it go too long, you risk starting over again. If that happens, and it probably could, begin again. The only time you fail is if you give up and revert back to your old habit.

Let yourself make mistakes along the way and learn what works and what doesn't. Changing a habit is about consistency. It's not about how much or how many, but how often. This is the frequency with which you take action.

If we expect perfection, we can also expect to fail. An all or nothing mindset often stops people from setting up new behaviors. I don't know of anyone who has a perfect track record. Habits take time and persistence, but most of all, patience. We have to be ready to forgive ourselves again and again. I have broken several bad habits this way, but in some cases it took years.

Habits are the thick strands of success built upon daily patterns of consistent practice and repetition of proven successful actions. These patterns make up the daily routines that mold an unbreakable cycle of conditioning. It is the consistent repetition of these key behaviors that builds the foundation for your life—the same patterns repeated over and over again, programming you for success, failure, or a mediocre existence.

You are the master programmer and architect of your own life. Habits are the tools you should master if you are to build the foundations of a good life."

The habit conversion formula is a powerful strategy for making permanent, lasting changes in your life by replacing non-constructive habits with those habits that are creative and contribute toward personal progress and development.

Many people are still operating on old programs using worn-out techniques and outdated systems that produce poor repetitive results. Your habits need a tune-up. This chapter is going to show you how to tune up your habits so you can squeeze the most out of your daily routine.

Your habits must support the dreams and goals you visualize for the future. If you are operating from a place of old thinking while trying to build a new way of living, you will meet incredible resistance. The habit conversion formula puts you on a new path of recovering and restoring your personal power. It focuses on lasting change, not just quick fixes, and sets you on the road to habit recovery.

It works on the old adage that everything in nature must have a balance. When we try to alter or convert a destructive habit, the habit must be replaced by its opposite element. Nature abhors a vacuum, and that which is removed must be replaced by something else of equal or greater value.

Balance is the key. If we change the weight on one side, we have to make it even on the other. The one reason people fail to change anything in their lives is because they don't really change anything at all. They only think they do. They might stop doing something altogether and then suffer withdrawals from the resistance of the habit as it struggles to become active again.

Stopping something cold turkey isn't changing it, just as starting something new and only following through with it once doesn't make it so. For example, people who have quit smoking and persisted didn't just sit around thinking about not smoking anymore. Those who did eventually started again.

Successful non-smokers became involved with life more than they ever had before, through physical exercise, eating better, using the money they would have spent on tobacco for vacations or building creative hobbies. Stopping smoking is not the reward; it is the habits you develop after you have stopped that make it worthwhile. This principal is applied to all habits that don't suit your needs.

A close friend of mine tried for over ten years to stop drinking. When he finally did, and someone asked him why it took so many attempts, he said, "Every time I stopped drinking I sat at home and thought about not drinking. I didn't realize it, but I was fueling the addictive habit by doing nothing. Once I started leaving the house and making active changes in my life, I didn't feel like a prisoner anymore. I was free."

The Habit Conversion Challenge Contract

At the end of this chapter is a habit conversion challenge sheet. You are going to use this to create new habits for lasting success. Fill out the form, answering the questions as completely as possible, and carry this contract with you wherever you go. Paste it in your workbook. Tack it on the wall. Put it wherever you can see it every day, to maintain a consistent level of focus and concentration.

How it Works

- Identify the current habit you are working on.
- Write down the habit you want to acquire. Why is this important?
- Follow this contract for a pre-determined number of days.

If you fail, start the contract over again. You are allowed to fail as many times as necessary.

Finally, don't give up!

Failure is part of the learning process. Be persistent! It is the key to succeeding. Habits build habits. Just remember, no matter what you want, no matter how impossible it may seem, there is always a way to overcome the adversity that opposes your efforts. There is always a way to succeed.

Habit Conversion Strategy Questions

Consider these questions when attempting to change the habits in your life:

- How does this new habit relate to your personal values and goals?
- What is the habit being converted?
- What is your plan of action? What are some simple steps you will take every day to succeed?
- What resources do you need to accomplish your goal?
- How will you reward yourself for succeeding?
- How will you feel after you succeed?

The Habit Conversion Challenge

The habit I want to replace is—

Example: I want to quit eating junk food.

The priority habit I will introduce to replace this is:

Example: I will eat more vegetables and read books about health.

Choose one habit that will be your priority. You will replace your old habit with this one.

The timeframe I will perform this replacement habit exercise is:

Example: 21 days, 30 days, or 45 days.

I recommend choosing a definite timeframe. If you are not satisfied with your results, you can reassess what you've done so far and try something new.

The changes I want to see through converting this habit are:

- Improved health
- Saving money that would be spent on junk food
- Weight loss
- Feeling better about myself

The methods (actions) I will use to convert this habit are:

- Replacing the craving for junk food with fruits and vegetables.
- Investing the money I save on junk food.
- Joining a gym and playing sports.
- Coaching others on the dangers of overeating fast food and junk meals.

What will happen if I don't change this habit, or if I give up changing it?

- I will suffer from obesity and digestive problems.
- I will lose all motivation to exercise and feel good about myself.
- Over the course of a decade, I will have spent well over $10,000 on junk food (calculated if I spent $3.00 a day for ten years).

Create Your Habit Conversion Contract

The habit I want to replace is:

The priority habit I will introduce to replace this is:

The time frame I will perform this replacement habit exercise is:

21 days —28 days — 30 days — 35 days — 42 days — 60 days

Write your answer here:

The changes I want to see through converting this habit are:

1.

2.

The methods (actions) I will use to convert this habit are:

1.

2.

What will happen if I don't change this habit, or I give up on changing it?

1.

2.

SECTION V:
Destiny of Wealth

"The only way to get love is to be lovable. It's very irritating if you have a lot of money. You'd like to think you could write a check: 'I'll buy a million dollars' worth of love.' But it doesn't work that way. The more you give love away, the more you get."

— **Warren Buffet**

Wealth is a
State of Mind

*"Money is multiplied in practical value
depending on the number of W's you control
in your life: what you do, when you do it,
where you do it, and with whom you do it."*

— Tim Ferriss

Depending on the scale and depth of your ambitions, making your greatest dreams come true might require you to have access to a few thousand dollars or several million.

Financing your lifelong dreams and objectives could involve something as simple as saving a few dollars a day or negotiating a deal with your bank or finance company to loan you a substantial amount. The ability to attract all the wealth that you will ever require is a valuable skill to making your vision and dreams a reality.

One day, you might find yourself trying to convince the right people that your plan for success is solid, regardless of whether the plan is to create a revolutionary product, construct a new building and hire staff for a new dynamic company, or design the world's most advanced theme park. Unfortunately, for many people, trying to come up with adequate financial resources to make the dream a definite reality poses a major obstacle.

The good news is that you don't have to be a financial wizard or stock market guru to obtain the cash to live the life you're seeking to experience. There is plenty to go around for everyone; you have to focus your thoughts on becoming wealthy and you will acquire the riches for achieving anything you want.

If you develop a rich consciousness and focus all your thoughts on gathering the necessary financial resources, all the wealth of the world is yours the moment you move from a mental state of hopelessness to developing a no-failure attitude.

The attainment of wealth isn't just about getting rich; it is how you attract wealth that matters most and constructing a positive mental attitude automatically brings wealth into your life.

A man with only twenty dollars in his pocket could amass a fortune if he has the wisdom and courage to put his money to good use. With a positive attitude and unshakable conviction in what you want to accomplish, the ability to attract riches lies in your mindset towards money and not in the hand that receives it.

Henry Ford and Andrew Carnegie are prime examples. These men amassed fortunes beyond their wildest dreams because of the power of their inner drive and a determination to see their vision become a reality. Absolute clarity about what they wanted to achieve was the secret to their fortune. The money was simply a result of that dream coming to life.

Mapping Your Road to Financial Freedom

Take a moment to think about the following questions. Write your answers in a notebook so you can refer to them later. This isn't a test. By answering these questions, you will be able to determine your financial situation.

Coming up with solid answers to these kinds of questions enables you to do something about your current financial situation. It moves you into a state of wealth consciousness, which in turn empowers you to begin attracting the level of wealth that you desire.

1. If you had access to $10,000 right now, how would you use it? How about $100,000? How about $10,000,000?

2. How important is money for you? What value do you place on having personal wealth?

3. How much of your salary do you actually save? How much could you save in five years if you put away $300.00 a month?

4. How many sources of income do you have? (Two part-time jobs/one full-time job/side business)

5. How much debt do you have? How does this restrict your current lifestyle? Are you limited or strapped down because of the amount of debt you owe? (Credit cards, financial loans to banks)

6. What investments do you have right now? Are these investments growing with each passing year? Do you know how much you made last year on your investments?

7. How much money will you need to finance your ultimate dream?

8. If you don't have this money right now, what is your plan for obtaining these funds? In case you don't have a plan for obtaining this money, what could you do to attract more money? Brainstorm this right now.

9. What beliefs do you hold about money? Do you believe that you are worthy of attaining financial freedom?

10. How old do you want to be when you can start living life in your own way? In other words, when do you want to

retire from making a living to making a life? Are you living that way right now?

11. What actions could you take today to get your mind focused on attracting and gaining more wealth?

12. How could having more money add value and quality to your life, community, and home?

13. If you could create your own business or develop a new product or brand, what would it be? What is the first step you could take right now to start moving in this direction?

14. How much money do you donate to charity? If you are not donating anything now, is there a charity you'd like to support? How much would you be willing to give right now? What is stopping you from doing this?

15. Do you have a fear of not having enough money? Does this fear stop you from taking risks or moving on new opportunities?

16. If your answer to question 15 is "yes," how would your life be different if you didn't have this fear holding you back?

17. How did you learn about saving and investing money? Who taught you?

18. Based on your current knowledge regarding money, what would you have done differently if you could?

19. What action could you take right now to increase your wealth and improve your current financial situation?

Almost everything in life costs money. We need money to fuel our quality of life. Whether you want to become self-employed, take a vacation, or purchase a dream house in Hawaii, the one thing I know for certain is that people who are able to finance their dreams enjoy a quality of life that is far superior to that of the average person working to make ends meet.

The process of building up your financial resources begins with creating a plan to enhance your level of financial awareness. The time and effort you spend today on planning your financial success for tomorrow will pay huge dividends in the future. Even if you do not become extremely wealthy, you will be far better off in ten to twenty years than if you were to do nothing and just coast along for the rest of your life.

A design for financial success doesn't just happen—you make it happen! Instead of being a slave to your money, you can become its master. Rather than feel helpless or hopeless, you can obtain financial freedom by developing a rich thought attitude. Once you believe you can have anything, you are ready to receive it.

Six Strategies for Building Wealth

"Many speak the truth when they say that they despise riches, but they mean the riches possessed by others."

– Charles Caleb Colton

1. Look out for the little stuff; it could be costing you a fortune

People are in the habit of spending their hard-earned money every day on stuff that seems trivial—candy, soft drinks, snacks, a new phone app, or coffee. This little stuff seemingly goes unnoticed because of the menial impact it has on our financial resources at the moment. After all, who really misses a dollar or two here and there?

Over a period of time, however, like the slow dripping faucet that goes unnoticed until it eventually creates a flood, this little stuff adds up to big dollars that you could be putting toward living your dreams. You may not notice the significance of throwing away a dollar today, but the amount of cash spent over the course of the next ten to twenty years could actually take you around the world and back.

Imagine that you're in the habit of buying coffee and a snack on the way to the office every day. This has been your routine for the past few years. This simple, harmless habit has been costing you approximately $3.00 per day, and because the amount is just "pocket change," you probably haven't noticed the difference. Assuming that it's only a few dollars a day, here's what it looks like when projected on a larger scale.

$3.00 × 1 day = $3.00

$3.00 × 365 days = $1,095 per year

At this point, I would like you to think about what you could do with $1,095. How much of a difference would it make if you had this amount in your savings account? Let's look at the next ten years:

$3.00 × 365 × 10 = $10,950

This is the cost of spending $3.00 per day over the course of ten years. Whether it is on snacks, lottery tickets, the newspaper, bottled water, or coffee, the little stuff really does add up to big cash.

Now, what could you do if you had $10,950? I can think of many things. You can either have your cake today and eat it, or discipline yourself to live without it and reap the benefits later. It's all up to you.

The purpose of this is not to make you feel guilty for stopping for coffee every morning or for treating yourself to a daily dose of ice cream. This is to show you the big picture over an extended period of time and how much money you could have if you managed to save it instead of spending $3.00 per day.

I know that $3.00 per day isn't much on the small scale of everyday life, but when it's put under a magnifying glass, you are actually spending a fortune every day. This is assuming that the amount spent on knickknacks is only $3.00. Many people spend an average of $10.00 per day.

Let's consider the total amount spent at the rate of $10 per day for five years:

$10.00 \text{ (a day)} \times 365 \text{ (days)} \times 5 \text{ (years)} = \$18,250$

Now that you can see what the little stuff adds up to, discipline yourself to only buy the things that you really need. Go for "bare bones" living and stop splurging. Don't give in to your cravings immediately. Remember that for every day you spend money on the little stuff, it's robbing you of the freedom you could have in the near future.

2. Put it in a safe place (the secret stash)

Years ago, I read a book that changed the way that I saved my money. It was The Wealthy Barber by David Chilton and it introduced me to a new concept: If you want to retire rich, you have to pay yourself before you pay anyone else. Although it made sense at the time, I didn't do it.

A few years later, I started reading David Bach's The Automatic Millionaire and his wisdom and advice took my knowledge of financial management to a whole new level. In the book, he emphasized the same concept I had read about years ago—pay yourself first!

I immediately heeded the advice, opened a separate account, and now every month, the money is automatically transferred from one account to another. I never see the transfer and I never do anything except work and let the bank move my money where I want it. It is this simple system that will eventually put a lot of cash in your hands. If you pay yourself first, you will be able to amass a small fortune over the course of ten, fifteen, or twenty years.

Imagine how much you will save if you automatically put away $200.00 per month. Do the math. Multiply this by twelve months and then again by twenty years. Before you even account for any interest, you already have $48,000 saved over the course of twenty years. This is a nice nest egg.

Develop an automated system for saving cash. Set yourself up with a save and stash system, let it grow, and someday you will be thankful you did. Even if you already have a pension plan, this is a separate account that you could have just for yourself. Think about all the wonderful things you could do with this cash.

If you only get a single idea from this chapter, I hope this is it. Visualize the vacation you're going to take, the dream house on the beach you're planning to buy, or simply working less so that you can spend more time with family and friends.

3. Control your debt

The personal debt accumulated over the years as a result of compulsive and excessive spending through credit cards and the interest on the principal amount has placed many people under significant financial stress, and in severe cases, caused complete financial ruin.

In today's world, anything is possible with the swipe of a card or an instant loan that pays for the things we want. The truth about accepting a loan is that unless you invest the money into something that is offering a return that is greater than its original value, you could be placing yourself in a vulnerable and financially regressive situation.

We have been led to believe that it is easier to play now and pay later. Why wait for the good things in life when you can have everything you ever wanted today? The concept of owning everything now and worrying about it later has become a way of life.

Many people have accumulated debts worth tens of thousands of dollars before establishing themselves in their careers or starting a family. If this is happening—or has happened—to you, there are several actions you can take to stop digging a financial hole. It's time for you to take control of your life and finances.

By controlling and managing yourself, you can avoid becoming burdened by the financial pressure of owing thousands with nothing to show for it. Here are some valuable suggestions to enable you to start controlling the amount of your debt accumulation every year.

a. Hold no more than one credit card.

Managing only one credit card is easier than attempting to juggle three or four bills every month. Owning several cards from multiple financial institutions (as most people do) makes it easier to slip further into debt, with multiple payments compounded by multiple interest rates.

The only winners here are the banks; you end up owing and eventually losing everything. By reducing your lifestyle to just one card, you can easily manage the expenditures and become more aware of what you are purchasing because you will have only one statement to review at the end of the month instead of a stack of bills.

You can also avoid using the card by stashing it at home. Only use it for special occasions. This will reduce your impulsive urge to use it every chance you get. By using only one card and keeping track of expenditures in a ledger, there will be no surprises when you receive your monthly statement.

b. Register one card online...only one.

If you shop online, register just one card as your primary source of payment. Having only one credit card bill enables you to track your purchases and the amount spent more easily than when you have several bills. Although registering several cards with eBay or Amazon gives you more shopping power and payment choices, it exposes you to the risk of falling deeper into debt.

The urge to purchase is greater when you have multiple payment choices and you can spread these payments around to balance the burden. These days, shopping online can offer terrific convenience, but it can also lead to financial ruin if you pay by multiple credit cards with excessive payments that go unnoticed.

c. Pay with cash whenever you can.

If you don't have the cash, put off making a purchase until you do. You will experience a deeper level of satisfaction that you applied personal discipline toward saving the money rather than just paying for it with a card and spending money you don't yet have. The belief that you can own it now and pay later is ruining your chances of financial freedom.

4. Make money from home

Walk through your house and make a list of all the things you own. Write down everything you can find, from antiques to stuffed toys. If you're like most people, you have accumulated items through birthdays, Christmases, and shopping sprees. Furthermore, most of the stuff you have spent years collecting is sitting in boxes, gathering dust and depreciating in value.

What if you could turn all your stuff into cash? Haven't you ever wished you could get your money back on something you bought on impulse, but knew it was too late to return? Unless something is a rare antique or a collector's item, you probably won't make more than half what you paid for it. Nevertheless, cleaning out your house or office could provide you with loads of cash if you do what millions of people are doing nowadays—selling their stuff online for cash!

A friend of mine recently made a list of everything in his house, set aside all the things he no longer used, and took pictures of all these items. Within a few weeks, he sold them all online and earned over $3,000.00. But this wasn't the end of it. He enjoyed selling online so much that he started an online business. As a result, he has doubled his monthly income.

You may be surrounded by items that are worth thousands of dollars without even knowing it. You could potentially take a trip, buy a new car, or put money in the bank for when you really need it.

For the next few days, walk through your home and take an inventory—paintings, silverware, clothes, toys, games, DVDs, collections, appliances, odds and ends, and even furniture. Make a complete list. Then, decide what you can sell. You could sell everything online, have a big yard sale, or enter a flea market. Either way, you will be able to pass along your unwanted stuff to others who need it.

Another option is to donate your stuff to a local charity or give it away to those who need it more than you do. You don't always have to make money to feel wealthy; a heart that is rich in giving is worth more than all the money you could make in a lifetime. There are plenty of charities to choose from. This will give you the opportunity to empty out your overflowing closets and fill up the lives of others who need your things more than you do.

5. Get wealth educated

Until a little less than five years ago, I knew almost nothing about saving, investing, or managing personal finances. I had never taken any kind of investment class and I had little knowledge about financial matters. By asking around, I discovered that most other people were just as financially uneducated as me.

In my days of high school (and maybe yours, too) dissecting a frog or learning about people who had been dead for hundreds of years was more important than training future generations to be responsible with money, teaching them how to invest or save, or educating them about a retirement fund.

It wasn't until several years ago that I decided that I no longer wanted to be stumped when it came to financial matters. If I was to start living my dreams, I had to get serious about saving and monitoring the cash that flowed in and out of my life every day.

After conducting some investigation, I discovered that the right source of information was crucial for financial education. I connected with people who understood finance. I found several authors who wrote books on the subject, and their research and techniques have helped countless people—including me—to understand the dynamics of personal finance.

If you desire to be financially educated, you have to be willing to invest the time and apply the necessary effort. Nobody is going to sit you down and give you the facts on how to save, spend, or earn more money. It's up to you to take the initiative! You have to educate yourself by reading the right books and talking with the right people. Put together a plan that is not only simple but also works for you.

You need to get access to the financial education that was never offered in school or by parents or friends, and once you are financially educated, teach what you know to others. Below, I have provided some recommendations to enable you to build your road to financial education and freedom.

Reading recommendations:

- *The Wealthy Barber* by David Chilton
- *The Science of Getting Rich* by Wallace D. Wattles
- *The Automatic Millionaire* by David Bach
- *Think and Grow Rich* by Napoleon Hill
- *The Total Money Makeover: A Proven Plan for Financial Fitness* by Dave Ramsey

6. Do what you love to do, and make money at it!

What if you could turn your hobby or favorite pastime into a real career? Imagine doing what you love and making money at it. How would you feel if you were making a million dollars a year doing something that you love, such as painting, writing, playing sports, or establishing a business? The people who experience an overall abundance of satisfaction are living the life they've always dreamed of because their passion is their livelihood.

If you want to experience complete fulfillment, make this your primary goal: Take what you love doing the most and make it your career. Whether you are an aspiring artist, writer, computer programmer, world-class adventurer, homemaker, public speaker, or just love to spend your free time creatively, you can live your dreams every day once you work out how to integrate your fun with your life's work.

The world is full of people living their dreams because they figured out how to turn their passions into a living. You can do what you love the most and get paid for it! Why should you have to wait until retirement to do what you want to do? Start your life right now so that your dreams can become your reality.

If you cannot integrate your deepest interests with your career path right now, make it your greatest passion to master your craft when you're not working nine to five. You will experience a freedom unlike any other when your passions become your source of wealth and fulfillment.

Wealth is 90% Attitude

Many people struggle to gain control of their financial freedom for several reasons. For one, they believe becoming wealthy is something beyond their means or ability. They feel they're not worthy of achieving any financial success. True wealth begins with our attitude toward money and the possibility of becoming financially successful.

In many cases, it is your beliefs about money that define your limitations. If you sincerely desire to become financially independent, you are going to have to realize that true wealth lies in the power of thought and attitude. Your beliefs about money and the thoughts and actions that follow are what attract wealth to you. If you believe you're rich, you are; if you believe you are poor, then you will be.

Bringing wealth your way doesn't require any special skills or abilities; you just need the proper attitude. By creating a wealthy attitude or mindset, you attract wealth. Just as a positive mind attracts wealth, a focus on limitations and beliefs that you'll always be "poor" repels the opportunity for building financial growth and gaining abundance.

One of the most common destructive beliefs is that we live in a world of limitations—limited resources, limited ideas, limited choices, and limited wealth. Too many people believe there simply isn't enough to go around and so we have to grab what we can, hold on to it as tightly as possible, and defend our limited abundance at all costs.

This attitude creates a life of scarcity and builds fear. Nothing could be further from the truth. We live in a world of abundance, yet many people choose to live like paupers. They clutch the scraps they've fought for, so nobody else can take them.

In the news, we are constantly bombarded with articles that support this fear of limited wealth and scarcity. According to recent news sources, the economy is bad, people are shopping less, jobs are being cut, and experts have predicted the next twenty years will be financially scarce. This causes many people to believe we don't have enough and never will.

When was the last time you read a positive article on the abundance available in the world? We are being fed the very beliefs that are keeping the world poor. We live in a limited world of insufficient resources, despite the colossal amount of wealth observed in our cities, towns, and even most of the average homes in first-rate countries.

Create Your Own Worth

Building wealth is a global effort. Imagine where we would be if everyone shared a similar positive attitude that they're as wealthy as they want to be. Don't ever let another person or a nation decide how much money you're worthy of having or making.

As we discussed earlier, you have the power of choice to create your own opportunity. You can live in scarcity for fear of never having enough or you can expand your creative and imaginative powers to build wealth beyond your wildest dreams. Build it first in your mind and you will attract all that you have ever desired into your life.

Instead of craving what you don't have, live each day as though you are already living in abundance. Those who hope and wish gather nothing, but the people who push their desires into the world attract all that they've ever wanted.

Do not permit thoughts of poverty or the media's negative predictions to destroy your abundant nature. Your new attitude of wealth is focused on creating abundance in all areas of life.

You already have everything you need to become rich and break free from the financial burdens of life through debt elimination. Now, educate yourself about your money and start putting it to good use. Believe that you are already wealthy, because you truly are!

SECTION VI:
The Pinnacle of Health

"To enjoy good health, to bring true happiness to one's family, to bring peace to all, one must first discipline and control one's own mind. If a man can control his mind he can find the way to Enlightenment, and all wisdom and virtue will naturally come to him."

— **Buddha**

Building Health and Maximizing Energy:
Eating the Right Foods

*"The way you think, the way you behave,
the way you eat, can influence your life by
30 to 50 years."*

— Deepak Chopra

You can follow all the great plans and do everything right, but if you fail to take care of your health, you won't be around to see the results of your planning. The last part of this book is about taking care of your health, and while it deserves a book of its own, there is enough material in this chapter to help you get started on staying in shape.

If you need to lose weight, improve your cardio, or recover from an illness, there are other books and courses you can utilize. Visit your local physician for advice, or speak to a health and fitness expert before trying a new exercise or diet regimen.

Eating Well

Exercising on a regular basis is a great way to keep the weight off while boosting self-confidence. After a good workout, you'll feel great. To take it a step further, exercise in combination with a healthy diet not only boosts the quality of your life but also reduces the risk of disease. People who focus on their physical activity and back it up by eating the right foods can outperform anyone regardless of age and function at their best performance levels every day.

Healthy people spend less time at the hospital, less money on medicine and health care, less time in bed, and miss less work. They tend to save more because they don't spend money on junk food or have unhealthy habits, such as excessive drinking, taking drugs, or smoking cigarettes. It's not my purpose to lecture about the dangers of these things; you are well aware of the risks involved. However, what I will do is cover some basics of nutritional eating.

In today's increasingly fast paced world, we may forget to take care of ourselves. Overeating—in addition to eating the wrong foods in the wrong combinations—can lead to the decimation of cells while poisoning the blood stream. As a result, we feel groggy and fatigued even after eight hours sleep and that feeling is accompanied by a loss of positive energy and enthusiasm.

Just as the mind and spirit require mental nourishment to operate at peak effectiveness, the body requires a source of energy to function at its fullest capacity. Your mind requires positive thinking to stay healthy. When your body and mind are well-nourished, this contributes to the overall value and happiness found in each day.

Fueling Your System

Just as a car runs on gasoline, a body that is nourished with the right foods will function longer, with increased mileage and little maintenance. If you load your system up with junk, you'll have less energy. To construct a sound body with mental and physical health, you need to focus on the quality of foods you take in as well as the size of the portions.

Knowing what to eat isn't sufficient enough; it is of vital importance to know *how much* to eat, and how to understand when your body has had enough. When we eat large quantities of foods from various food groups, the body breaks everything down and sorts it out. Some foods, such as fruits and vegetables, are digested and absorbed by the stomach quickly and efficiently.

Other foods take longer to break down and depending on how much you have eaten and in what combinations, the process requires considerable energy and time to digest everything. Have you ever felt completely exhausted after eating a huge meal? This is because your body is using its energy to break down all the complicated stuff that just went into your system.

Eating the foods we want and in large quantities feels enjoyable. However, after repeating this pattern for years and without giving any thought to the quality or quantity of the diet—not to mention the strange hours of the day that some people eat—our pleasure eventually turns to pain. This can result in stomach indigestion, heart disease, and obesity.

It is hard to believe that if we're not responsible, the food we eat can kill us someday. Remember the foods you consume can either improve the quality of your life, or completely ruin it. Whatever you eat, and how much, will impact how you feel.

If you're in the habit of eating loads of junk, you will feel sluggish. If you eat nutritious greens with the right amount of carbohydrates and proteins, you will feel ready to do anything. One style of eating gives you vital energy; the other approach kills this energy.

The key is to create healthy eating habits that support the lifestyle you desire. If you build these habits today, you will not only extend your life but you will improve the quality of your life.

The Habit of Eating Well

"The higher your energy level, the more efficient your body. The more efficient your body, the better you feel and the more you will use your talent to produce outstanding results."

– Anthony Robbins

Food supplies the body with energy. This energy is used as an efficient means to repair and maintain the functions of the physical body. When you supply your body with proper foods, such as vegetables, fruits, and a balance of meat and carbohydrates, you are essentially programming the body to perform its most vital functions at peak levels. Likewise, food that is low in nutrition and protein and high in fat, or is comprised of artificial products, will deplete the body of the energy it requires.

Eating well is a habit. However, before it can become a habit, you have to know what and how much to eat. In today's world of information technology, advanced levels of research and experiments constantly provide us with updates and new results on what is and isn't good and what does and doesn't work. Something that was once considered to reduce the chances of cancer now contributes to it; foods once thought to be harmful are now accepted as a part of a daily diet.

It's easy to get caught up in all the research and massive amounts of information regarding today's healthy way of living. It doesn't have to be difficult, and in fact, it really isn't. There are simple programs to follow and most of the information is readily available in books, on television, or on the Internet.

You don't have to be reminded that smoking kills and excessive abuse of substances, such as alcohol or drugs, shortens your life and weakens your organs. We know this, just as we are aware that the daily consumption of a healthy dose of vegetables and fruits extends your life, keeps the body clean, and leaves you feeling energetic and ambitious.

Reduce Your Intake

You do not have to eat large quantities out of habit or force; in fact, most people can get by on eating only sixty percent of what they normally consume. There's nothing to gain by eating a large meal at eight p.m. and then sitting down to watch TV for two hours. If you have ever done this—and I have—you might have awoken the next morning with that same food still in your stomach, barely feeling hungry.

Your body and your stomach has been asleep, so it hasn't had a chance to digest anything. Moreover, if you ate a heavy dinner, such as rice or meat and potatoes, it probably won't be fully digested until the next morning.

There's nothing wrong with eating below your hunger level. We eat when we're hungry or when it's time for dinner, and we usually eat until we've stuffed ourselves. You could actually eat only sixty percent of what you normally do and you would feel better and be just as active. More food is not always good. Massive food consumption causes the death of thousands of people every year.

The key is to listen to your body and not your mind. What is it telling you? What do you think it's craving? The mind is deceiving; its cravings are only based on the desire to consume. Have you ever found yourself eating even after your stomach was full? Your body didn't need the extra food, but the mind convinced you to eat. When you reach for a piece of cake or chocolate instead of fruit, is it your body that wants it, or is it the mind? Compulsive eating habits can create as much mayhem as any other habit.

Recommended healthy food intake includes fresh fruit and vegetables, meat, and dairy products. If you're a vegetarian, ensure you get enough protein through other means, such as beans and eggs. Avoid large quantities of junk.

Ten Power Tips for Healthy Eating

Power Tip #1: Eat plenty of vegetables and fruits every day. Include a dark green vegetable, such as broccoli, asparagus, or romaine lettuce, and an orange vegetable, such as carrots or sweet potatoes.

Power Tip #2: Every day, half of your consumption of grain products should be whole grain, such as brown and wild rice, bulgur, quinoa, or oatmeal.

Power Tip #3: Fish is high in protein and has little fat and few calories. Eat fish twice a week and you will keep your system clean while adding protein to your diet.

Power Tip #4: Include beans, lentils, and tofu (meat alternatives) more often in your diet. These are easily digested and are a terrific source of energy and vitality.

Power Tip #5: Drink lower fat milk and milk alternatives, such as fortified soy beverages. Be aware that other fortified drinks such as orange juice, and foodstuff such as rice, almonds, and potatoes, do not contain the same level of protein found in milk or soy.

Power Tip #6: Use unsaturated oils, such as canola, olive, and soybean as well as non-hydrogenated margarines. Include a small amount in your diet each day: 30 to 45 ml/2 to 3 tbsp.

Power Tip #7: Take a vitamin D supplement if you are over the age of fifty. Vitamin D, also known as the sunshine vitamin, is synthesized when sunlight hits the body. Vitamin D improves bone mineral density and builds stronger bones. A healthy intake of vitamin D lowers the risk of some cancers, multiple sclerosis, and reduces the risk of injury from falls or accidents.

Power Tip #8: Eat slowly. Take your time when eating. This helps with digestion and you'll enjoy your food more. People who eat too fast usually end up with indigestion and a stomachache.

Power Tip #9: Drink enough water. It's one of the best habits for cleaning out your system and keeping it operating at maximum performance. You don't have to drown yourself by drinking too much water, but remember to drink water when you're thirsty as opposed to bottled juice or a soft drink.

Power Tip #10: Eat breakfast every day! I believe breakfast is, as they say, the most important meal of the day. Also, the quality of the foods you eat in the morning sets the pace for the rest of the day.

If you eat a healthy mixture of fruits, your body will digest it easily and provide the greatest return in energy as water-based food. Fruits should be eaten on an empty stomach, as they are digested best this way. Fruit should never be eaten when you are completely full.

Building Health and Maximizing Energy:
Breathing

Try this simple exercise. Take a deep breath, hold it for three seconds, and then slowly exhale. Repeat this process. Now, inhale once more and hold your breath for four seconds, exhaling slowly. Feel your lungs fill up with air. Visualize the oxygen entering your system, moving through the bloodstream, and being transported to all your vital organs.

Breathing effectively is a vital part of being healthy. Surprisingly, most of us neglect the way we breathe. We are not consciously aware of it as we go about our daily business. However, taking the time to focus on deep breathing several times a day will greatly enhance your overall feeling of well-being.

Breath of Life: The Importance of Breathing

Deep breathing in itself is a form of exercise. By doing so, you are giving the body what it wants the most—oxygen! Engaging in three to five sessions of deep breathing every day improves blood circulation and increases your body's vitality and energy.

Breathing properly begins with an awareness of your breathing patterns. By breathing full, complete breaths, you can significantly improve your overall health. Your breathing patterns are influenced by many factors, particularly your emotional state.

When you feel stressed, angry, fearful, or anxious, your breathing is affected. For example, when you are under immense stress, you might hold your breath without realizing it or when you are anxious, you may reduce your breathing to short rapid bursts.

Have you ever experienced difficulty breathing when you're stressed? Alternatively, have you ever held your breath in moments of great fear or anxiety? When you lose touch with your breathing and permit the situation or emotion to control your breathing patterns, the increase in stress causes you to breathe in shallow, short gasps. If this is prolonged over time, it causes a buildup of toxins in the body and blocks the bloodstream that carries healthy oxygen to the cells.

Breathing Exercise

It is vital that you become aware of your breathing patterns. Partaking in mindful breathing exercises each day will considerably improve your physical vitality by contributing to building and sustaining healthier cells for a more efficient bloodstream.

Breathing properly also clears your mind and reduces stress. It heightens your senses, giving you a feeling of peace. Practicing deep breathing several times a day at regular intervals can reduce and control your stress levels, fatigue, anxiety, irritability, and muscular tension resulting from prolonged activity.

Here are some suggested exercises to help you to relax and control your breathing. You can do these exercises at home while watching TV, at the office during your lunch break, in a coffee shop, or while commuting to work on the bus or train.

Imaginative Breathing Exercise: Deep and Relaxed Breathing

This breathing exercise combines the power of autosuggestion and imagination with deep breathing. In other words, together with breathing deeply, you will use your imagination to cleanse your mind and build a positive mental state.

Begin by sitting up straight in a relaxed position. Your hands should be kept in a resting position on your legs.

Breathe in deeply. As you breathe in, think about something that makes you happy. This could be a goal you're working toward, a quote you may have heard, or a memory of spending time with someone you care about. Hold this image in your mind and continue breathing.

Imagine that as you inhale, you are drawing positive energy toward you through each breath, and as you exhale, the negative energy is being pushed away from you. Try this for ten minutes.

Breathe in deeply for a count of three; exhale on the count of four. Inhale again and repeat the same steps.

As you inhale, feel the oxygen as it enters your lungs. When you exhale, imagine yourself pushing out all the negative energy, as well as physical and mental contaminants that have built up inside your body. This is as much a mental exercise as a physical one. Repeat these steps six to eight times in every session. I recommend doing this twice a day—once in the afternoon and once at night before bed.

Building Health and Maximizing Energy:
Physical Exercise

Besides eating well and breathing effectively, the third focal point is exercise. When you nourish the body by consuming healthy food, you build up a storehouse of energy that is released as soon as physical activity is applied.

Years ago, I discovered the benefits of lifelong dedication to physically training my body. Regular exercise will not only enable you to keep the weight off, but you will also look good and feel great while building a storehouse of physical energy so that you can function at peak levels for maximum performance and efficiency.

There are many different forms of physical training. Some people prefer playing sports, whereas others enjoy yoga. There's bodybuilding or aerobics, swimming, running, or speed walking. Regardless of what you prefer, engaging in some form of activity at least twice a weak considerably boosts your energy levels.

A consistent exercise routine also builds confidence and contributes to the overall quality of your life. A balance of aerobic activity, light muscle training, and regular stretching with focused breathing techniques is all you need to build a solid physical foundation.

Aerobic Activity

Any exercise that concentrates on expanding the cardiovascular system is known as aerobic training, which includes swimming and running.

Whenever you perform an activity that creates the need for oxygen, it can be classified as an aerobic activity. Depending on the intensity of the exercise, it is categorized as moderate intensity or vigorous intensity aerobic exercise.

Aerobic Exercise in Moderation

Aerobic activity, when performed in moderation over a period of time, has the following benefits:

- Burns fat
- Increases the level of oxygen intake
- Increases the metabolic rate
- Creates a stronger and more efficient immune system
- Generates more energy
- Reduces the risk of heart disease by preventing the clogging of arteries
- Enhances performance in all areas of life
- Creates a foundation of learned discipline as the body is conditioned to stay in shape
- Enhances the body's ability to distribute oxygen to all vital organs

It takes approximately four to six months of consistent aerobic activity to build a strong, healthy foundation. If your exercise routine is irregular, you will fail to gain the real benefits of aerobic activities.

For example, the benefit you'll get from running or swimming occasionally will be much less than what you can achieve by performing the same exercise consistently twice a week for six months. To make improvements, a regular routine is essential. It takes months of moderate exercise to develop a strong aerobic state.

If you were training for a triathlon, you wouldn't start running, swimming, and biking all in the same week. Doing so would only result in muscle injury and cause more harm than good. The key is in moderation over a sustained period.

Exercise is no different than practicing the piano; if you want to become a good pianist, you have to have a regular routine of practice. Over time, you'll develop the skills for the long term. Therefore, the key to staying healthy is to make exercise a part of your life. Make exercising regularly a priority for the long-term.

Consistent practice and making moderate adjustments to your exercise routine as you become stronger and more capable of handling a heavier physical workout is the key to success. Make your workouts a regular habit and keep altering your routine so that you don't become bored or stagnant.

Moderate / Low-Intensity Exercise

This form of physical activity accelerates the heart rate and makes you breathe harder. It includes riding a bicycle, speed walking, or playing light sports that don't involve rigorous movements or extended running.

This type of exercise is fun and can be performed for an extended period over several hours with a lower heart rate. Although your breathing is hard, you can talk. In this state, you are burning oxygen, which creates a good aerobic condition. You will be able to burn fat more easily and generate a high level of sustained energy.

Vigorous / High-Intensity Exercise

This includes any sport or exercise that makes the heart race faster. By playing football, soccer, or basketball and being in constant motion, you burn sugar and stored fat.

It is recommended that you do not start training by throwing yourself into vigorous exercise. Your body needs to be conditioned to build up to a vigorous activity level. The intensity of this type of exercise needs to be altered according to age, as well.

Warming Up, Cooling Down, and Eating After

Warm up before exercise

The most common injury in sports is caused by a lack of stretching beforehand. A pulled muscle is often a result. One of the best ways to warm up before any exercise is to spend ten to fifteen minutes stretching. These are generally low-impact exercises to prepare the body for physical activity.

When you do this, focus on your breathing. Draw in deep breaths for a three-second count and exhale for four seconds. This expands your lungs and enhances your workout by improving the body's endurance ratio.

Cooling down

Cooling down after exercise is just as important as warming up, and it is a vital part of concluding a workout. This gives the body time to make the transition from a state of rapid exertion to a state of relaxation. The process of cooling down allows the body to normalize the breathing and heart rate.

During this phase, focus on light movements, such as stretching or walking. As we discussed earlier, this is a good time for breathing exercises, too. Finally, drink a glass of water to rehydrate.

Focus on eating complex carbohydrates before a workout.

Glucose is your body's most essential source of fuel. Your pre-workout meal should be comprised of complex carbohydrates. Ensure this is a small meal, and wait at least one hour for the food to be converted into energy to be used while training.

If you are doing moderate aerobics, just a light snack with a short waiting time before exercise is sufficient. For complex workouts, eat carbohydrates with a light protein combo, and lengthen your waiting period. Bread, vegetables, or pasta are recommended food items for a pre-workout meal.

Post-workout meal

The meal consumed after exercise is as important as the meal consumed before the workout. First, you should typically try to eat within an hour after your training, and make it proteins and carbohydrates. Avoid fats of any kind. Eating fats in this phase slows the digestion process of the carbs and proteins.

The size of this meal depends on your body weight. For more information, visit Canada's Food Guide. It will provide you with a more detailed approach, complete with tables and a personal tracking system for recording everything you consume.

The Workout Box

During the next week, you are going to record the food you eat. Note how you feel after the food you consume. Are you full of energy or do you feel sluggish? Did you have a balance of vegetables today? What time did you eat dinner, and what did you eat?

By listening to your body and your stomach, you can gauge how certain foods affect you. You can keep track of what and how much you eat by using "My Food Guide Servings Tracker" in the Canadian Food Guide.

Workout Plan and Training – If you check the Internet or your local bookstore, you will find a wide resource of workout routines and schedules for just about anything you're interested in. It really depends on how you want to exercise and what you want to do.

Another alternative is to visit your local gym and see what they have to offer. Although you can generally train for free at home without spending money, many people like the motivational atmosphere of going to a gym. You can also get a free consultation on training and dieting. Set up a workout routine that coincides with your health and fitness goals.

Conclusion

"Keep your dreams alive. Understand to achieve anything requires faith and belief in yourself, vision, hard work, determination, and dedication. Remember all things are possible for those who believe."

— **Gail Devers**

Drive Your Destiny Home

"Nothing brings me more happiness than trying to help the most vulnerable people in society. It is a goal and an essential part of my life - a kind of destiny. Whoever is in distress can call on me. I will come running wherever they are."

— Princess Diana

Your life is shaped by choice—not by circumstances or by the constantly changing events around us.

We can choose whether or not to believe, whether or not to act, or whether or not to live a freedom-rich lifestyle. We can choose our actions, and the actions we take define our character.

You are not defined by circumstances. But as I discussed in this book, you can create the circumstances you want. If you're not happy, it's your mission to change that. Do you want more love, more money, and more freedom? All of this is attainable, but it's not easy to get if you don't believe in your ability to achieve. You want more freedom? You have to take the right actions to attain it.

This book is about forging choices, taking action, and best of all, making a difference. Nothing can be more rewarding than believing in yourself and creating powerful alliances with those who support you, whom you can support in return.

Destiny is not a one-person mission. It is collaboration as we work together to make this world a better place.

You can have what you want, if you really want it. Then, you can get more of it by helping others get what they want.

As motivational entrepreneur Zig Ziglar once said, "You can have everything in life you want, if you will just help other people get what they want."

Make Your Impact

A life is meant for living. We are dynamic creatures born to explore, dream, love, and contribute the best of ourselves to this life. If we are not living our dreams and crafting the life we want, then what are we here for?

Live in the moment. People get into the habit of expecting the future to be better than the present. Do you ever find yourself wanting life to hurry up so you can get to the next milestone? Do you feel impatient because you haven't achieved what you desire yet? Do you know what you'll do once you get there?

The only time that exists is the moment you're in right now. Your destiny isn't always something that's happening several decades down the road. Your destiny is being lived right now. Take a moment to contemplate all the opportunities coming your way today.

What could you do right now to live a dynamic, fearless lifestyle?

Why wait to live? There is nothing to guarantee that you'll be happier, richer, or healthier than you are today.

Be mindful of what you can do today. Will you take more trips? Greet more people? Make more friends? Exercise regularly? Be happier just because you can? Be less fearful and more energetic?

Live while you are here. Live with passion and look for every moment to stay awakened. Be mindful that time is limited and there is so much you can enjoy. Spread your joy with others. Show them the fruits of a life well-lived, because there are too many out there who have lost their way and they have given up on living. You can show people how to live again and embrace the limited time we are all given.

Listen to your calling. This is the voice that nobody except you can hear. If you listen, you will know your purpose, and you can find a way to make it happen. This is knowing that something in your life is acting on your behalf to bring you everything you've ever desired.

Be the author of your own life. We are all authors on the journey of life. You are the author of the greatest adventure on earth—your own life! Your life is a story being told every day. Each moment weaves a story of the ongoing saga of your life. It's up to you to make it a bold and daring journey.

As the author of your own life story, you can shift things by controlling your thoughts. By making decisions and acting on your thoughts and intuitive feelings, you can apply the mystery of your imagination to create the situations you want to experience.

If you think your life is boring, think again. There's no such thing as a boring life, only a boring storyteller. You have the mighty pen in your hand, and with it, you hold the key that unlocks the secrets to life. People who write their own scripts live the way they want to. They don't let others do the storytelling for them.

In order to write your life the way you want, you have to know what you want. You will never have the ending you desire if you don't decide on your goals. Although we cannot control a lot of what happens in our lives due to situations beyond our control, we can decide what we would like and work toward the desired outcome. For this to happen, your story must be told your way.

Your life is a series of chapters with endings, beginnings, and in-betweens. If you think you need a change in your life, you decide what should be changed. When you start a new chapter, this doesn't mean the story ends.

A new one is beginning and it continues onward, unfolding in ways you never imagined before. One door closes and another opens. Finish one chapter and start the next one. Keep moving on and grow with each new page of your life.

Now that you have finished this book, you have everything you need to develop your own story for living an amazing life. If you are looking for a miracle, remember that you are the miracle.

A Final Word...

I just want to say thank you.

Thank you for being you and for joining me on this trip. If you stick to it, I have a lot more to show you.

Before we come to the end of this book, just know that I really appreciate you traveling with me. I hope we have the chance to meet someday. But until then, you can stay in touch with me via email: scott@scottallanauthor.com

You can also connect with me here on my blog to receive weekly blog posts on how to empower your life, develop fearless confidence, and build your dreams from the ground up.

Don't let your dreams go unanswered.

Focus on the quality of living and not the quantity. It isn't about living longer but living better. Take risks and do what scares you. Don't hold back on something just because your fear tells you it's a bad idea.

Discover your real passion and commit right now to living out the rest of your days doing what you love with people you love. There is no better way to live than to share, contribute, dream, learn, grow and live your life with impact.

Why do we wait for life to start? The future you are waiting for is now, and the only one who can take action toward your dreams is you.

The best time to start is today.

Live. Love. Embrace the moment. Believe in your journey.

I'll see you again soon, on the other side.

Scott Allan

About Scott Allan

Scott Allan is a bestselling author who has a passion for teaching, building life skills, and inspiring others to take charge of their lives. Scott's mission is to give people the strategies needed to design the life they want through choice.

He believes that successful living is a series of small, consistent actions taken every day to build a thriving lifestyle with intentional purpose. By taking the necessary steps and eliminating unwanted distractions that keep you stuck, you are free to focus on the essentials.

Scott Allan lives in western Japan and is currently working on several new writing projects.

You can connect with Scott online at:

www.scottallanauthor.com

Email: scott@scottallanauthor.com

Empower Your Thoughts: How To Convert Great Ideas into Successful moneymaking Ventures

Empower Your Fear: Leverage Your Fears To Rise Above Mediocrity and Turn Self-Doubt Into a Confident Plan of Action

Empower Your Life: The 9 Timeless Principles to Unlock Your Purpose, Fulfill Your Destiny and Supercharge Your Success

Rejection Reset: A Strategic Step-By-Step Program for Restoring Self-Confidence, Reshaping an Inferior Mindset, and Thriving In a Shame-Free Lifestyle

Rejection Free: How To Choose Yourself First and Take Charge of Your Life By Confidently Asking For What You Want

Do It Scared: Charge Forward With Confidence, Conquer Resistance, and Break Through Your Limitations

Relaunch Your Life: Break the Cycle of Self-Defeat, Destroy Negative Emotions, and Reclaim Your Personal Power

Confidence
Coaching Program
with Scott Allan

*Life waits for no one. It's time to stop struggling alone and **take action**.*

Are you stuck in life?

Looking for action-focused solutions to creating a thriving lifestyle?

Are you tired of the same old routines taking you nowhere?

Are you ready to turn your life's passion into a reality and start living the life you want?

If yes, **then it's time to do something about it.** The time has come for you to hire a coach and mentor.

When you hire me as a coach, we will work together to help you achieve three main goals:

1. Break down your fears and develop a program to take action.
2. Discover your greatest passion and how to do what you love.
3. Overcome the self-defeating behaviors that are holding you back.

4. Take massive action toward your goals.

Every session is **custom tailored** to match your specific needs and goals. Your obstacles will be defeated and together we can figure out your next move. If you are truly committed to making changes, now is the time.

By working with me and committing to making positive life changes, you will be able to:

- Identify the limiting beliefs, thoughts, and behaviors holding you back.
- Identify who you are and the values and goals that matter to you.
- Identify core issues and the solutions to remove confusion and uncertainty.
- Develop better relationships with people you care about.
- Create a personalized plan for your future.
- Put an end to being passive and charge forward with greater confidence.
- Learn the strategies that world-class entrepreneurs practice to overcome adversity.
- Face your fears and build the confidence to do anything scared. (No matter how scared you are.)
- Put real strategies into play so that you can maximize your coaching sessions.
- Get unstuck and move forward with the next BIG step in your life.
- Find that hidden niche in your life and channel your creative energy into doing what you love.

To learn more, contact me directly at scott@scottallanauthor.com or use the contact form at http://www.scottallanauthor.com.

Don't wait for life to show up and give you what you want. You need a vision, a plan, and a coach to help you get there.

Let me help you shape your **life's passion** into a **thriving journey**.

Scott Allan is a **bestselling author** and **personal development trainer**. His books and course material help people create the life they want to lead. You can find out more at www.scottallanauthor.com

> "The journey of a thousand miles begins with one step."
> — **Lao Tzu**

Made in the USA
Coppell, TX
24 January 2020